Performance, Risk and Competition in the Chinese Banking Industry

CHANDOS
ASIAN STUDIES SERIES

Series Editor: Professor Chris Rowley,
Centre for Research on Asian Management, Cass Business School,
City University, UK; HEAD Foundation, Singapore
(email: *c.rowley@city.ac.uk*)

Chandos Publishing is pleased to publish this major Series of books entitled *Asian Studies Series*. The Series Editor is Professor Chris Rowley, Director, Centre for Research on Asian Management, City University, UK and Director, Research and Publications, HEAD Foundation, Singapore.

Asia has clearly undergone some major transformations in recent years and books in the Series examine this transformation from a number of perspectives: economic, management, social, political and cultural. We seek authors from a broad range of areas and disciplinary interests: covering, for example, business/management, political science, social science, history, sociology, gender studies, ethnography, economics and international relations, etc.

Importantly, the Series examines both current developments and possible future trends. The Series is aimed at an international market of academics and professionals working in the area. The books have been specially commissioned from leading authors. The objective is to provide the reader with an authoritative view of current thinking.

New authors: we would be delighted to hear from you if you have an idea for a book. We are interested in both shorter, practically orientated publications (45,000+ words) and longer, theoretical monographs (75,000–100,000 words). Our books can be single, joint or multi-author volumes. If you have an idea for a book, please contact the publishers or Professor Chris Rowley, the Series Editor.

Dr Glyn Jones
Chandos Publishing
Email: *g.jones.2@elsevier.com*

Professor Chris Rowley
Cass Business School, City University
Email: *c.rowley@city.ac.uk*
www.cass.city.ac.uk/faculty/c.rowley

Chandos Publishing: Chandos Publishing is an imprint of Elsevier. The aim of Chandos Publishing is to publish books of the highest possible standard: books that are both intellectually stimulating and innovative.

We are delighted and proud to count our authors from such well-known international organisations as the Asian Institute of Technology, Tsinghua University, Kookmin University, Kobe University, Kyoto Sangyo University, London School of Economics, University of Oxford, Michigan State University, Getty Research Library, University of Texas at Austin, University of South Australia, University of Newcastle, Australia, University of Melbourne, ILO, Max-Planck Institute, Duke University and the leading law firm Clifford Chance.

A key feature of Chandos Publishing's activities is the service it offers its authors and customers. Chandos Publishing recognises that its authors are at the core of its publishing ethos, and authors are treated in a friendly, efficient and timely manner. Chandos Publishing's books are marketed on an international basis, via its range of overseas agents and representatives.

Professor Chris Rowley: Dr Rowley, BA, MA (Warwick), DPhil (Nuffield College, Oxford) is Subject Group leader and the inaugural Professor of Human Resource Management at Cass Business School, City University, London, UK, and Director of Research and Publications for the HEAD Foundation, Singapore. He is the founding Director of the multi-disciplinary and internationally networked Centre for Research on Asian Management (*http://www.cass.city.ac.uk/cram/index.html*) and Editor of the leading journal *Asia Pacific Business Review* (*www.tandf.co.uk/journals/titles/13602381.asp*). He is well known and highly regarded in the area, with visiting appointments at leading Asian universities and top journal Editorial Boards in the UK, Asia and the US. He has given a range of talks and lectures to universities, companies and organisations internationally with research and consultancy experience with unions, business and government, and his previous employment includes varied work in both the public and private sectors. Professor Rowley researches in a range of areas, including international and comparative human resource management and Asia Pacific management and business. He has been awarded grants from the British Academy, an ESRC AIM International Study Fellowship and gained a 5-year RCUK Fellowship in Asian Business and Management. He acts as a reviewer for many funding bodies, as well as for numerous journals and publishers. Professor Rowley publishes extensively, including in leading US and UK journals, with over 370 articles, books, chapters and other contributions.

Performance, Risk and Competition in the Chinese Banking Industry

Yong Tan

ELSEVIER

AMSTERDAM • BOSTON • CAMBRIDGE • HEIDELBERG • LONDON
NEW YORK • OXFORD • PARIS • SAN DIEGO
SAN FRANCISCO • SINGAPORE • SYDNEY • TOKYO
Chandos Publishing is an imprint of Elsevier

CP
CHANDOS PUBLISHING

Chandos Publishing
Elsevier Limited
The Boulevard
Langford Lane
Kidlington
Oxford OX5 1GB
UK
store.elsevier.com/Chandos-Publishing-/IMP_207/

Chandos Publishing is an imprint of Elsevier Limited

Tel: +44 (0) 1865 843000
Fax: +44 (0) 1865 843010
store.elsevier.com

First published in 2014

ISBN: 978-1-84334-765-1 (print)
ISBN: 978-1-78063-446-3 (online)

Library of Congress Control Number: 2014949851

British Library Cataloguing-in-Publication Data.
A catalogue record for this book is available from the British Library.

Project management by Neil Shuttlewood Associates, Gt Yarmouth, Norfolk, UK
Printed in the UK and USA

Contents

List of figures and tables

Figures

Tables

List of abbreviations

ABC	Agricultural Bank of China
ADBC	Agriculture Development Bank of China
AMC	Asset Management Company
BIS	Bank for International Settlements
BCC	Banker–Charnes–Cooper
BOC	Bank Of China
BOCOM	Bank Of COMmunication
CAR	Capital Adequacy Ratio
CBRC	China Banking Regulatory Commission
CCB	China Construction Bank
CCBs	City Commercial Banks
CCR	Charnes, Cooper, and Rhodes
CDB	China Development Bank
CEIB	China Export–Import Bank
CRS	Constant Return to Scale
DEA	Data Envelopment Analysis
DMU	Decision Making Unit
EXIM	EXport–IMport Bank of China
GLS	Generalized Least Squares
GMM	General Method of Moments
ICBC	Industrial and Commercial Bank of China
IPO	Initial Public Offering
JSCB	Joint Stock Commercial Bank
LLPTL	Loan Loss Provision over Total Loans
NIM	Net Interest Margin
OLS	Ordinary Least Squares
PBC	People's Bank of China
PBT	Profit Before Tax
PTE	Pure Technical Efficiency
ROA	Return On Assets

ROE	Return On Equity
SCP	Structure–Conduct–Performance
SE	Scale Efficiency
SFA	Stochastic Frontier Approach
SME	Small and Medium size Enterprise
SOCB	State-Owned Commercial Bank
SOE	State-Owned Enterprise
TFP	Total Factor Productivity
TSM	Trusted Services Manager
UCC	Urban Credit Cooperative
VRS	Variable Return to Scale
WTO	World Trade Organization

Acknowledgements

I would like first to express my gratitude to my PhD supervisor, Dr Christos Floros, who was responsible for turning my interest into enthusiasm not only for research in the Chinese banking industry but also for further work in academia.

I would also like to thank Professor Tim Coelli, who gave me permission to reproduce some of his work in my book.

Special thanks also go to Professor Chris Cowton, Dean of the Business School at the University of Huddersfield, and to Dr John Anchor, Head of the Department of Strategy, Marketing and Economics at the Business School. The friendly academic environment at the Business School significantly improved my work efficiency and further contributed to completion of the whole work.

I would also like to express my gratitude to Dr Glyn Jones, George Knott, and Harrier Clayton at Chandos, as well as the book's project manager, Neil Shuttlewood, who provided strong support during my writing process.

Last but not least, I would like to express my deepest gratitude to my parents: Lianmin Tan and Jie Liu. Thank you ever so much for your consistent patience, guidance, help and encouragement during my eight years of study in the UK. Any achievement I have made would not have been possible without you. This book is not mine – it belongs to the two of you.

Preface

As the largest developing country in the world, economic development in China is attracting great attention across the globe. The banking sector, an important component of the financial system, plays a vital role in promoting the economic development of the whole country. In other words, a sustainable banking sector provides the basics for a well-developed economy. Several rounds of banking reforms in China have aimed to improve bank performance, increase competition and enhance the stability of the banking sector. The government and banking regulatory authorities are concerned about such issues as: How well are Chinese commercial banks performing? Have the conditions for competition in the Chinese banking sector improved? Has the Chinese banking sector become more stable?

The book comprehensively examines how the Chinese banking sector performed between 2003 and 2011. As a result of there being different ownerships of Chinese commercial banks, this book also evaluates the conditions for competition in the Chinese banking sector over the period in question. Not only are the conditions for competition examined on a year-by-year basis, but interbank competition in different bank ownerships is also investigated. Because of the 2007 financial crisis, the risk-taking behaviour of Chinese commercial banks (stability of the Chinese banking sector) has been closely scrutinised by government officials and banking regulatory authorities. The book focuses on this issue. Investigation of the impact risk has had on the performance of Chinese commercial banks coupled with the influence competition has had on the risk-taking behaviour of Chinese commercial banks (stability of Chinese banking sector) are special features of this book.

Chapter 1 mainly deals with the content covered by each chapter of the book.

Chapter 2 reviews the banking reforms brought about by the Chinese government. The structure of the Chinese banking sector is then presented. Finally, there is an overview of the Chinese banking sector over the period in question, in which the total assets, market shares, non-performing loans and non-performing loan ratios among state-owned commercial banks, joint stock commercial banks, city commercial banks and foreign banks are presented, compared, and discussed.

Chapter 3 discusses corporate governance in the banking sector. It starts by reviewing the different definitions of corporate governance. Theories relevant to corporate governance are then discussed, and the corporate governance problems facing banks are presented. Finally, bank corporate governance in practice is discussed.

Chapter 4 investigates the impact risk has on performance in the Chinese banking sector. The chapter begins by looking at the theory of bank performance. There then follows a review of the relevant literature on Chinese bank performance. The methodology used to measure bank risk and performance, as well as the method used to investigate the impact risk has on bank performance are then explained. The chapter finally presents and explains the results.

Chapter 5 examines the conditions for competition in the Chinese banking sector. Much like Chapter 4, the chapter begins by looking at the theory of bank competition. The methodology used to estimate bank competition is then discussed. This is followed by a review of the literature on competition in the Chinese banking sector. Findings on the conditions for competition in the Chinese banking sector and the impact competition has had on the risk-taking behaviour of Chinese commercial banks are finally presented and discussed.

Chapter 6 discusses further development in the Chinese banking sector and focusses on such issues as setting up an equitable and fair salary system, internationalization, the growth of urbanization, capital replenishment, maintaining and improving innovative capacity as well as implementing the Basel III Capital Accord.

Chapter 7 summarizes the book and proffers a number of useful conclusions.

Overall, *Performance, Risk and Competition in the Chinese Banking Industry* is the first book to examine the state of the Chinese banking sector so comprehensively. The book could be used as a banking course in universities. The Chinese government and China's banking regulatory authorities could also find the book useful when assessing policy implications.

About the author

Yong Tan, PhD, is Lecturer in Economics at the Business School of the University of Huddersfield, UK, which won the Times Higher Education Award for the University of the Year 2013. Before joining the Business School, he was a part-time Lecturer in Economics at the University of Portsmouth Business School, UK. The author has experience of teaching various modules in various areas of economics and finance for both undergraduate and postgraduate students such as Economics for Business; Macroeconomics; Microeconomics; Econometric Methods; International Trade and Payments; Money, Banking and Finance; and International Economics.

The author is originally from China and has spent eight years studying and living in the UK. He finished his BA(Hons) in International Business English, MSc in Business Economics, Finance and Banking, and PhD in Economics at the University of Portsmouth. While studying for his PhD, he published a number of academic papers about the Chinese banking sector in a number of well-known international journals including *Journal of International Financial Markets, Institutions and Money*; *Journal of Economic Studies*; *Journal of Emerging Market Finance*; *Journal of Developing Areas*; *Economic Issues*; *Studies in Economics and Finance*; and *Journal of Chinese Economics and Business Studies*. Furthermore, he acts as a reviewer for various economics and finance journals on a regular basis and has presented research papers at international conferences.

1

Introduction

Abstract: The Chinese economy underwent significant growth between 2003 and 2011. As an important part of the economy, the banking sector plays an important role and its performance is being paid a great deal of attention by government officials, banking regulatory authorities, bank managers and academic researchers. The Chinese banking sector has undergone several rounds of banking reforms since 1978, the purpose of which was to increase competition and improve stability. This book investigates not only the performance, risk and competitive conditions in the Chinese banking sector, but also the relationship among them, and in so doing provide policy implications to the government. This chapter will provide background information on the Chinese banking sector and the structure of the whole book will be outlined as well.

Key words: introduction, structure of the book.

Introduction

The financial system around the world has undergone significant changes over the last three decades. Banking output in terms of providing various financial services can be done using fewer inputs as a result of deregulation, globalization, financial innovation and technological progress. In other words, technical efficiency has significantly improved in the banking sector. However, the banking sector in developing countries, China especially, suffers from a higher level of government control which in turn leads to lower bank competition and inefficient allocation of resources. Furthermore, as argued by Garcia-Herrero et al. (2009), the Chinese banking sector remains undercapitalized, saddled with non-performing loans and profitability is below international standards. The Chinese government has implemented several rounds of banking reforms in order to create a more competitive environment and improve efficiency and stability in the banking sector.

The economic reform that has been ongoing in China since 1979 has the purpose of transforming the planned economy into a socialist market economy. As the most important component of the country's economy, the banking sector in China has undergone a number of reforms including creating a two-tier banking system, establishing three policy banks to separate state-owned commercial banks (SOCBs) from policy lending, encouraging banks to be listed on stock exchanges to obtain external monitoring, and relaxing the requirements for foreign banks to enter Chinese markets. The objectives of these measures taken by the Chinese government are to improve the performance of Chinese banks in terms of profitability, efficiency and productivity, and at the same time create a more competitive environment and strengthen stability in the banking sector. Assessing profitability, efficiency, competition and their determinants has policy implications for the government and banking regulatory authority regarding further reforms that need to be initiated.

Corporate governance is an important area that is widely discussed in both non-financial firms and banking sectors. Chapter 3 provides a discussion of bank corporate governance by first defining corporate governance and then overviewing the theories relevant to corporate governance. Three important theories are discussed: agency theory, stakeholder theory and stewardship theory. The chapter also discusses the corporate governance problems that banks have to face by explaining corporate governance structure, government safety nets, opaqueness and market competition. The chapter then turns to the topic of bank corporate governance in practice by discussing ownership structure and governance, and the topic of internal governance.

Chapter 4 examines the relationship between bank risk and bank performance in the Chinese banking sector over the period 2003–11. The risk facing Chinese commercial banks is measured by the ratio between loan loss provisions and total loans. To check the robustness of the results, two alternative risk indicators are used: the Z-score[1] and stability inefficiency. This is believed to be the first study to use these two risk indicators of bank performance in China. The ratio of loan loss provisions to total loans and the Z-score provide the risk conditions of Chinese state-owned, joint-stock and city commercial banks, while the estimation of stability inefficiency provides the risk conditions of the whole Chinese banking sector over the examined period. In terms of bank performance, three different performance indicators are used: bank profitability, bank efficiency and bank productivity. The four profitability indicators used are return on assets (ROA), return on equity (ROE), net interest margin (NIM) and profit margin (PBT or profit before tax). As far as the estimation of bank efficiency is concerned, the non-parametric data envelopment analysis (DEA) CCR and BCC models are used to derive technical efficiency, pure technical efficiency and scale efficiency, while output-oriented DEA is used to measure bank productivity. Besides the impact risk has on bank performance, this chapter also controls for comprehensive bank-specific, industry-specific and macroeconomic determinants of bank performance. The bank-specific determinants include bank size, liquidity, capitalization, overhead cost, non-traditional activity and labour productivity. Banking sector development, stock market development and banking sector concentration are three industry-specific variables that are controlled for. Both the GDP growth rate and the inflation rate are included as macroeconomic determinants of bank performance. In terms of econometric estimation, the Generalized Method of Moments (GMM) system estimator is used. This chapter starts off by explaining the theories of bank profitability, bank efficiency and bank productivity and then discusses the determinants that affect bank profitability, bank efficiency and bank productivity. The chapter goes on to review the literature on bank profitability, bank efficiency and bank productivity in China. The chapter also looks at the methods used to estimate bank risk as well as the determinants of bank profitability (GMM), bank efficiency, bank productivity and the impact risk has on technical efficiency (Tobit[2] regression). After some descriptive data there is a presentation and discussion of empirical results as well as some concluding remarks.

Chapter 5 examines the competitive conditions that prevailed in the Chinese banking sector between 2003 and 2011. Its focus is the impact of competition on the risk-taking behaviour of Chinese banks. The three-bank concentration ratio,[3] the Lerner index[4] and the Panzar–Rosse H statistic[5] are the competition indicators used. The three-bank concentration ratio and the Panzar-Rosse H-statistic are used to measure the competitive conditions of the Chinese banking sector on a year-by-year basis over the examined period, while the Lerner index provides the competitive conditions of three different types of ownerships of Chinese banks: state-owned commercial banks, joint-stock commercial banks and city commercial banks. To check the robustness of the results, the ratio of loan loss provisions to total loans, Z-scores and the stability inefficiency are used as risk indicators. Comprehensive bank-specific and macroeconomic variables affecting bank risk are controlled for such as bank size, bank liquidity, non-traditional activity, overhead cost, GDP growth rate and annual inflation rate. The chapter begins by explaining the theory of bank competition including the structure–conduct–performance theory, Lerner index and Panzar-Rosse H-statistic, and then goes on to estimate the level of bank competition and model the impact of competition on risk-taking behaviour. The chapter then reviews the literature on competitive conditions in the Chinese banking sector and looks at hypotheses regarding the impact of competition on bank risk. The chapter then presents and discusses the empirical results. Finally, there is a conclusion and summary.

After examining the performance of and competitive conditions in the Chinese banking sector in Chapters 4 and 5, Chapter 6 discusses further developments in the Chinese banking industry. In the chapter our discussion focusses on the following issues: stimulation given to the Chinese banking industry, internationalization of the Chinese banking industry, the impact the growth of urban construction has had on Chinese commercial banks, capital replenishment of the Chinese banking sector, the latest on the innovation capacity of Chinese commercial banks, implementation of the Basel III capital accord. The chapter ends with a summary and conclusion.

Chapter 7 summarizes and concludes the book.

Notes

1. The Z-score is a formula used to predict bankruptcy. It was the brainchild of Edward I. Altman, a Professor of Finance at New York University.
2. The Tobit model is named after James Tobin. It describes the relationship between a non-negative dependent variable and an

independent variable. It is a combination of truncating "Tobin" and adding "-it" by analogy with the probit model.

3. The concentration ratio measures the percentage market share held by the largest firms in an industry.
4. The Lerner index describes the market power a firm has. It was formalized by Abba Lerner in 1934.
5. The Panzar–Rosse H-statistic is used to measure competition.

2

The evolution, reform and development of the Chinese banking sector

Abstract: Since the late 1970s, a series of banking reforms have been implemented by the Chinese government to improve the performance, enhance the stability, and create a more competitive environment in the banking sector. This chapter will start by reviewing banking reforms since 1979 and then review the structure of the Chinese banking sector. This will be followed by an overview of the Chinese banking sector over the period 2003–11 with emphasis on different indicators such as market share of assets, volume of non-performing loans and non-performing loan ratios, and capital adequacy and profitability of different ownerships of commercial banks.

The chapter is structured as follows: "China's banking reforms" reviews Chinese banking reforms that have taken place over the last three decades. "Structure of the Chinese banking sector" looks at the structure of the Chinese banking sector with a focus on the introduction of banking regulatory authority and different ownerships of commercial banks. "Overview of the Chinese banking sector over the period 2003–11" and "Summary and conclusion" bring the chapter to an end.

Key words: Chinese banking reform, structure of Chinese banking, overview of Chinese banking.

China's banking reforms

As an important component of the financial system, the banking sector plays an important role in the development of the country's economy. In order to have a healthy and well-developed banking sector, the Chinese government has implemented a series of reforms that can be split up into three periods: the first covering 1979 to 1994, the second from 1994 to 2001, and the last covers the period since 2001 when China joined the WTO.

The Chinese socialist banking system was established in the late 1940s along the lines of the system in the former Soviet Union. The central bank, the People's Bank of China (PBC), was founded in 1948 by consolidating the former HuaBei Bank, Beihai Bank, and XiBei Peasant Bank. PBC was stripped of its central bank functions during the Cultural Revolution (1966–76), but later regained responsibility for currency issue and monetary control.

Prior to the economic reform in 1978, the Chinese banking industry was a mono-banking system, where the PBC combined the roles of central and commercial banking. Other banks – which were either taken over/restructured into the PBC or under administration by the PBC or the Ministry of Finance – were just part of the hierarchy ensuring that national production plans would be fulfilled and that there was no incentive to compete with one another. Since 1978, a number of reforms have been gradually implemented by the Chinese government in order to improve performance and create a more competitive environment in the banking sector (Yao et al., 2007).

A two-tier banking system was established during the first reform period which lasted from 1979 to 1984 with the purpose of improving banking services given to state-owned enterprises and increasing bank productivity. The first tier of the banking system is the PBC, the central bank of China, which has the responsibility of supervising the operation of various financial institutions such as all specialized banks, non-bank financial institutions, and insurance companies. The second tier of the banking system, on the other hand, mainly comprises four newly established stated-owned commercial banks: the Bank of China (BOC, established in 1912), the China Construction Bank (CCB, established in 1954), the Agricultural Bank of China (ABC, established in 1979), and the Industrial and Commercial Bank of China (ICBC, established in 1984). During this period these four state-owned commercial banks served as the lending arms of the government; they made loans to state-owned enterprises in order to fulfil the state plan under government direction. More specifically, each of these four state-owned commercial banks was responsible for credit allocation in specific economic sectors. For instance, the ABC mainly provided financial services to the agricultural sector, while the CCB made loans to help fund infrastructure projects and urban housing development. The ICBC provided financial support to help fund commercial and industrial activity in urban areas, and the BOC focussed its business on foreign exchange and foreign business transactions. To make it easier for local enterprises to get credit, various branches and local offices were established in different provinces around the country. The operation of these branches is governed by local authorities rather than the central bank. The function of these branches/offices is to help local governments fulfil their production plans and, hence loans are made to state-owned enterprises with no consideration given to profitability.

As a result of state-owned enterprises in China at this time being highly inefficient and making massive losses every year from their operations, the loan provision of state-owned commercial banks to these enterprises increased bank risk and the higher rate of loan default rate built up the number of non-performing loans. Furthermore, as discussed earlier, each of these four state-owned commercial banks provided loan services to specific economic sectors; despite having strong market power in their own designated areas there was no competition among the four banks. In order to increase competition among these four banks and achieve the goal of establishing a market-oriented economy, the four state-owned commercial banks were allowed to make loans to any economic sector without any restriction after 1985. They competed with each other in various areas such as loan and deposit services, fund raising and capital allocation, but the competition at this stage was very limited because there were no foreign banks in the Chinese banking industry and, more importantly, central and local government were still heavily involved in banks' operations (Yao et al., 2007).

In an effort to reduce the high number of non-performing loans in the Chinese banking sector, especially those of state-owned commercial banks, three policy banks were established in 1994 by the Chinese government to take over policy-leading responsibilities: the China Development Bank (CDB); the China Export–Import Bank (CEIB), and the Agriculture Development Bank of China (ADBC). They are funded by issuing bonds and accepting some deposits; they are wholly owned by the government. Their purpose is to accomplish the country's policy of industrial and regional development. Unlike the other institutions mentioned above, they have not been set up to make profits. More specifically, the CDB mainly provides loans to government-invested projects related to infrastructure and pillar industries; while the CEIB mainly supports government in terms of providing loans to help the export and import of capital goods; last but not least, the ADBC mainly funds state-invested projects like agricultural development in rural areas.

Two important banking laws were enacted in 1995: the Law of the People's Bank of China and the Commercial Bank Law. The Law of the People's Bank of China was enacted to define the status and functions of the People's Bank of China, ensure the correct formulation and implementation of monetary policy, establish and improve the macroeconomic management system of the central bank, and maintain financial stability. Furthermore, it stipulates that the People's Bank of China shall be under the leadership of the State Council and is free from intervention by local governments, government departments at various levels, non-governmental organizations, and individuals. The Commercial Bank Law was formulated to protect the legitimate rights and interests of commercial banks, depositors and other clients, standardize the behaviour of commercial banks, improve the quality of funds, strengthen supervision and administration, ensure the safety and soundness of commercial banks, maintain good financial order, and promote the development of a socialist market economy. The establishment of these two laws not only formalizes the operation of Chinese commercial banks, but gives commercial banks more autonomy in terms of credit allocation. Although the policy-lending activities of state-owned commercial banks were taken over by policy banks, central and local government still allocate policy-lending tasks to state-owned commercial banks.

The barriers to entry for new banks have been relaxed by the PBC ever since the mid-1980s, the purpose of which was to increase competition in the banking sector. Joint stock commercial banks (JSCBs) started to be set up and operate nationwide, the aim of which was to maximize profits. In 1987 the Bank of Communication (BOCOM) was established and became the first JSCB in China.[1] Several other JSCBs established in the late 1980s and early 1990s include the CITIC Bank, China Merchant Bank, Shenzhen Development Bank,[2] China Everbright Bank, Industrial Bank, Guangdong Development Bank,[3] Huaxia Bank, Evergrowing Bank and Shanghai Pudong Development Bank. Two JSCBs were established in 1996: Bohai Bank and Minsheng Bank. The most recent JSCBs to be set up in China include Evergrowing Bank and Shanghai Pudong Development Bank, which were established in 2003 and 2004, respectively.

Unlike the big four state-owned commercial banks (SOCBs) which are wholly owned by the Chinese government, most JSCBs in China mainly comprise the shares of two parties: local government/state-owned enterprises and foreign banks. Unlike SOCBs, JSCBs enjoy relatively more freedom and less government intervention, hence the belief that JSCBs have healthier asset quality, higher profitability, and a lower number of non-performing loans.

Apart from JSCBs, a number of urban credit cooperatives and rural credit cooperatives were established as well at the beginning of 1990s. They finance small and medium-sized rural and urban enterprises and individuals. As a result of local government investing the funds to establish cooperatives, government officials have absolute control over the operations of cooperatives. Bribes from a number of high-risk firms/companies induce government officials to put pressure on cooperatives to make loans to them, which leads to a buildup in the number of non-performing loans. In accordance with State Council regulation, urban credit cooperatives have been gradually transforming to city commercial banks since 1995, while rural credit cooperatives have been gradually changing to rural commercial banks since 2001.

China's entry to the World Trade Organization (WTO) marked the beginning of a new era for the Chinese banking industry and the prospect of fierce competition with foreign banks. To comply with its WTO commitment, the Chinese banking sector gradually opened up to higher competition from foreign financial institutions and the ban on foreign banks offering currency business in China was gradually removed. More specifically, by the end of 2001 foreign banks were allowed to offer foreign currency business to Chinese and foreign enterprises and individuals all over the country, but they were only allowed to offer local currency business to foreign enterprises and overseas citizens in specific cities such as Shanghai, Shenzhen, Dalian, and Tianjin. By the end of 2002 the restriction was loosened further and foreign financial institutions could offer local currency business in Guangzhou, Nanjing, Qingdao, Wuhan, and Zhuhai. By the end of 2003 more cities were opened up to local currency business by foreign financial institutions including Ji'nan, Fuzhou, Chengdu, and Chongqing. Furthermore, it was possible to offer local currency business to all Chinese and foreign enterprises and overseas citizens. By the end of 2004 the list of cities expanded to include Beijing, Xiamen, Kunming, Shengyang, and Xi'an. By the end of 2005 Ningbo, Shantou, Harbin, Changchun, Lanzhou, Yinchuan, and Nanning were added to the list. Foreign financial institutions were treated exactly the same as domestic banks regarding the provision of local currency business by the end of 2006.

Four asset management companies (AMCs) were established by the Chinese government in 1999 with the purpose of reducing the number of non-performing loans of the Big 4 SOCBs. They were Cinda, Oriental, Great Wall, and Huarong. The original idea was to assign one AMC to each state-owned commercial bank with Cinda going to the China Construction Bank; Oriental to the Bank of China; Great Wall to the Agricultural Bank of China and Huarong to the Industrial and Commercial Bank of China. The amount of non-performing loans from the four SOCBs written off by AMCs reached RMB1.4 trillion in 1999–2000, which reduced the non-performing loan ratios of the SOCBs by 10 per cent. In other words, the non-performing loan ratio decreased from 35 to 25 per cent. There were two further write-offs of non-performing loans by the four AMCs in 2004 and 2005. In 2004 non-performing loans worth RMB278.7 billion from the Bank of China and the China Construction Bank were purchased by Cinda and then, in

2005, non-performing loans worth RMB142.4 billion from the Bank of China, RMB56.9 billion from the China Construction Bank, and RMB64 billion from the Bank of Communication were purchased by Oriental and Cinda. These purchases reduced the number of non-performing loans of Chinese state-owned banks. Financial asset management corporations are subject to regulations and are supervised by the PBC, the Ministry of Finance, and the State Securities Supervisory Committee of China.

The China Banking Regulatory Commission (CBRC) was established in March 2003 with the purpose of increasing the efficiency of regulatory and supervisory functions in the banking sector. Its establishment freed up the central bank of China – the PBC – to focus on its role in China's macroeconomic management. The CBRC is under the control of the State Council. Two laws came into effect in 2005 with the purpose of improving the performance of and stability in the Chinese banking sector: The Law of the People's Republic of China on the People's Bank of China and The Law of the People's Republic of China on Commercial Banks.

Regulation Governing Capital Adequacy of Commercial Banks, a new rule regarding the capital adequacy level of Chinese commercial banks, was promulgated by the CBRC in February 2004 in order to improve risk management and enhance stability in the Chinese banking sector. Formulation of the rule was based on combining the 1998 Basel Capital Accord (Basel I) and the 2002 Basel Capital Accord (Basel II). The Commercial Bank Law enacted in 2005 has a clause requiring commercial banks to keep a minimum capital adequacy ratio of 8 per cent, while the new rule complements the law by providing a mechanism for calculating the capital ratio of commercial banks. The new rule further stipulates that all commercial banks need to meet the minimum capital adequacy ratio of 8 per cent before 1 January 2007.

The computation procedure implemented by the new rule increases the capital adequacy ratio (CAR) of commercial banks by an average 2 per cent compared with the old rule (Basel I). In other words, the new rule imposes stricter requirements on the capital adequacy level of Chinese commercial banks. Further requirements imposed by the regulatory authorities ask Chinese banks to establish risk management structures and a rating system. As a consequence, based on the new Basel Capital Accord (Basel II), new internal rating and credit risk management systems were developed by the Big 3 state-owned commercial banks: the Bank of China (BOC), the China Construction Bank (CCB), and the Industrial and Commercial Bank of China (ICBC).

According to the Finance and Insurance Enterprise Financial Regulation established by the Ministry of Finance in 1993, Chinese commercial banks classified loans into four categories before 1998: normal loan, past due loan, doubtful loan, and bad loan. According to this system, non-performing loans consist of past due loans, doubtful loans, and bad loans. This classification emphasized the payment status of a loan rather than its risk assessment. In May 1998, in accord with international practice and China's national conditions, the PBC formulated loan classification guidelines requiring Chinese commercial banks to classify loans into five categories according to borrowers' capabilities of repaying the loans: normal, special attention, sub-standard, doubtful, and loss. Although this new loan classification was introduced in 1998, it was not fully implemented by Chinese commercial banks until 2003. Compared with the four-category loan system, the new classification emphasizes risk assessment. Normal and special attention loans belong to performing loans, while non-performing loans include sub-standard, doubtful, and loss loans.

Apart from the four AMCs, The Pilot State-owned Bank Overhaul Program was initiated by the State Council in 2003. As indicated by the title of the program, it was mainly oriented toward state-owned commercial banks and the purpose was to inject fresh capital, resolve the issue of non-performing loans, and improve corporate governance. The first two state-owned banks enrolled in this program were the BOC and the CCB, which had capital injections of USD 22.5 billion split between them in December 2003. BOCOM and ICBC were the second group of banks to get capital injections from the government. More specifically, the Chinese government injected capital worth RMB3 billion to BOCOM in 2004 and capital worth USD 15 billion was injected to the ICBC in 2005. The capital injections substantially reduced the non-performing loans of these banks.

In order to improve risk management and acquire fresh capital, all Chinese banks are encouraged to attract foreign strategic investment. In other words, the Chinese government welcomes foreign investment in domestic Chinese banks. The regulation regarding foreign equity investment in Chinese financial institutions was issued by the CBRC in December 2003. The regulation stipulates that a single foreign investor cannot hold more than a 20 per cent ownership stake in a local bank, while total foreign investments can be up to 25 per cent of the total equity of one domestic Chinese bank. Thus, foreign investors are allowed to take minority ownership in Chinese financial institutions. As a result of their involvement in bank operations, Chinese banks can benefit from more risk management experience. From 2003 to 2007, a time when the major Chinese banks were restructuring, there was a boom in foreign investment in China. By the end of 2008, 24 Chinese banks including the 4 state-owned commercial banks,[4] 9 JSCBs[5] and 11 city commercial banks held investments from 29 foreign strategic investors (Hasan and Xie, 2012).

To improve the efficiency and corporate governance of Chinese banks, all banks are encouraged to be listed on stock exchanges. The first bank making an initial public offering (IPO) was the Shenzhen Development Bank, which was listed on the Shenzhen Stock Exchange in 1991. In June 2005 BOCOM successfully made its IPO on the Hong Kong Stock Exchange, becoming the first Chinese domestic bank listed overseas. In October 2005 the CCB successfully made its IPO on the Hong Kong Stock Exchange, becoming the first listed state-owned commercial bank in China. Another two state-owned commercial banks, BOC and ICBC, made their IPOs on the Hong Kong Stock Exchange in June and October 2006, respectively. Offshore markets are preferred by the Chinese government because it considers overseas markets stricter than the domestic market in terms of information disclosure, something the Chinese government believes is critical to promoting structural reform and improving the efficiency of Chinese banks. In order for domestic banks to obtain more capital from domestic investors, the BOC, ICBC, and CCB were listed on the Shanghai Stock Exchange as well in July 2006, October 2006, and September 2007, respectively. The last state-owned commercial bank, the ABC, was listed on both the Hong Kong and Shanghai stock exchanges in July 2010. By the end of 2011 a total of 16 Chinese commercial banks were listed on stock exchanges.

Structure of the Chinese banking sector

Banking authorities

There are two regulatory authorities in China's banking system: the People's Bank of China (PBC) and the China Banking Regulatory Commission (CBRC). Both are governed by the

State Council of the People's Republic of China. The PBC was established on 1 December 1948. The State Council decided to have the PBC function as the central bank in September 1983. The main functions performed by the PBC are (1) to formulate and implement monetary policy in accordance with the law; (2) to issue the Renminbi and administrate its circulation; (3) to regulate financial markets, including the inter-bank lending market, the inter-bank bond market, the foreign exchange market, and the gold market; (4) to prevent and mitigate system financial risks to safeguard financial stability; (5) to hold and manage the state's foreign exchange and gold reserves.

So that the PBC can concentrate on monetary policy issues, its banking regulation and supervision function was taken over by the CBRC, which was established in 2003. The main functions of the CBRC include (1) formulating supervisory rules and regulations governing banking institutions; (2) authorizing the establishment, changes, termination, and business scope of banking institutions; (3) conducting on-site examination and off-site surveillance of banking institutions and taking enforcement actions against rule-breaking behaviour. The regulatory objectives of the CBRC include (1) protecting the interest of depositors and consumers and maintaining market confidence through prudential and effective supervision; (2) promoting financial stability and enhancing the international competitiveness of the Chinese banking sector.

Five large-scale commercial banks

The Big 4 SOCBs are the Agricultural Bank of China (ABC), the China Construction Bank (CCB), the Industrial and Commercial Bank of China (ICBC), and the Bank of China (BOC). They are commonly known as the Big 4. As lending arms of the government they mainly make loans to state-owned enterprises (SOEs) in specific sectors of the economy. However, with the establishment in 1994of three policy banks in China to conduct policy-lending responsibilities directed by the Chinese government, the SOCBs started engaging in consumer and commercial businesses. Due to the fact that SOCBs provided credit to SOEs at a time when most of them were not profitable, the buildup of non-performing loans in SOCBs resulted in constraints on their earnings and profitability. In 2006 BOCOM was officially defined as a state-owned commercial bank by the CBRC, together with the Big 4; there are five SOCBs in China's banking sector. A special supervision department was set up by the CBRC to oversee the operation of these five SOCBs. At the end of 2011, the total assets of the five SOCBs reached RMB53,633.6 billion, 12.57 per cent higher than the figure in 2010. However, the five SOCBs' assets as a proportion of total banking industry assets fell to 47.34 per cent in 2011 which is much lower than the previous year (49.2 per cent). In spite of this, these five SOCBs are and will continue to dominate China's banking system.

Agricultural Bank of China

The predecessor of the Agricultural Bank of China (ABC) was the Agricultural Cooperative Bank established in 1951. On 15 January 2009 the bank was restructured into a joint stock limited liability company. Capitalizing on its comprehensive business portfolio, extensive distribution, and advanced IT platform, the bank provides various corporate and retail banking products and services for a broad range of customers. At the end of 2011, it had 441,144 employees across 23,624 branches and banking offices in mainland China, two overseas branches in Hong Kong and Singapore, and five representative offices in New York, London, Tokyo,

Frankfurt, and Seoul. According to its annual statement, the total assets of the bank reached RMB11.7 trillion at the end of 2011. Its total deposits and total loans reached RMB9.62 and 5.63 trillion in 2011, respectively. In addition, the operating profit achieved in 2011 was RMB122 billion with a growth rate of 22.2 per cent over the previous year. The capital adequacy ratio achieved 11.94 per cent, while the non-performing loan ratio was 1.55 per cent.

China Construction Bank

中国建设银行 China Construction Bank

The China Construction Bank (CCB) was originally established in 1954 when it was charged with the administration and allocation of government funds for construction and infrastructure-related projects. The CCB became a fully commercial bank in 1994. Its business scope mainly includes providing corporate banking, personal banking, treasury operations, and various products and services (such as infrastructure loans, residential mortgages, and banking card business). On 27 October 2005, the bank made its IPO on the Hong Kong Stock Exchange and on 25 September 2007 it was successfully listed on the Shanghai Stock Exchange. At the end of 2011, it had 329,438 employees across 13,581 branches and banking offices in mainland China, 9 overseas branches located in Hong Kong, Singapore, Frankfurt, Tokyo, Seoul, New York, Johannesburg, Sydney, and Ho Chi Minh City. According to information released by the bank, its total assets were RMB12 trillion at the end of 2011, while total deposits and total loans were 10 trillion and 6.5 trillion in 2011, respectively. In addition, the operating profit for 2011 was RMB169 billion, representing a growth rate of 25.48 per cent over the previous year.

Bank of China

The Bank of China (BOC) was established in February 1912, making it the oldest bank in China. After formation of the People's Republic of China, the BOC became a specialized foreign exchange and international trade bank, giving significant support to foreign trade development and economic infrastructure by offering international trade settlement, overseas fund transfer and other non-trade exchange services. In August 2004 Bank of China Limited was established and then listed on the Hong Kong and Shanghai stock exchanges in June and July 2006, respectively, becoming the first Chinese commercial bank listed on both the mainland and Hong Kong. As the most internationalized and diversified bank in China, BOC provides a full range of financial services on China's mainland as well as in Hong Kong, Macau, and another 31 countries. It mainly engages in commercial banking including corporate banking, personal banking, and financial market business. It also conducts investment banking as well as insurance services, fund management services, direct investment, investment management, and aircraft leasing services. At the end of 2011 the total assets of the bank were RMB11.83 trillion, while its total liabilities were RMB11.07 trillion, representing growth rates of 13.1 and 13.19 per cent over the previous year. The non-performing loan ratio of the bank was 1.00 per cent, a decrease of 0.1 per cent over the previous year. Operating profit increased by 18.81 per cent reaching RMB130.3 billion in 2011 compared with 2010.

Industrial and Commercial Bank of China

The Industrial and Commercial Bank of China (ICBC) was established on 1 January 1984 and was restructured into a limited liability company on 28 October 2005. On 27 October 2006, ICBC successfully made its IPO on both the Shanghai and Hong Kong stock exchanges. At the time it was the world's largest IPO with a value of USD21.9 billion.

By dint of the hard work of its staff and stable development, ICBC has become the world's most valuable and profitable listed bank and is the No. 1 bank in the world in terms of the amount of deposits. It has 16,648 outlets in mainland China, 239 overseas subsidiaries, and 1,669 representative offices. At the end of 2011, its net profit was RMB208.4 billion, representing a growth rate of 25.6 per cent over the previous year. The total loan value of the ICBC at the end of 2011 reached RMB7.79 trillion , representing a growth rate of 14.7 per cent over 2010, while the total deposits of the bank were RMB12.26 trillion, representing a growth rate of 10 per cent over the previous year. The total assets of the bank at the end of 2011 were RMB15.48 trillion, a growth rate of 15 per cent compared with 2010. The non-performing loan ratio at the end of 2011 was 0.94 per cent, a decrease of 0.14 per cent over 2010.

Bank of Communication

交通银行 BANK OF COMMUNICATIONS

The Bank of Communication (BOCOM) was founded in 1908, making it one of the oldest banks in China. It is currently one of modern China's note-issuing banks. In June 2005 and May 2007 it was listed on the Hong Kong and Shanghai stock exchanges, respectively.

The bank provides a range of financial services including commercial banking, brokerage services, trust services, finance leases, fund management, insurance, and offshore financial services. It has three wholly owned subsidiaries: Bank of Communication International International Holdings Co. Ltd, China Bank of Communication Insurance Co. Ltd and Bank of Communication Finance Leasing Co. Ltd.

It also has controlling interests in a number of subsidiaries including Bank of Communication Schroder Fund Management Co. Ltd, Bank of Communication International Trust Co. Ltd, BoCommlife Insurance Co. Ltd, Dayi Bocomm Xingmin Rural Bank, Zhejiang Anji BOCOM Rural Bank Ltd, Xinjiang shihezi BOCOM Rural Bank and Qingdao Laoshan BOCOM Rural Bank. In addition, the bank is the largest shareholder of Jiangshu Changshu Rural Commercial Bank Co. Ltd. At the end of 2011, the total assets of the bank were RMB4.6 trillion and net profit was over RMB50.7 billion, representing growth rates of 16.9 and 29.95 per cent, respectively, while total deposits and loans were RMB3.28 trillion and RMB2.56 trillion, representing growth rates of 14.48 and 14.52 per cent, respectively, over the previous year. The non-performing loan ratio was 0.86 per cent at the end of 2011, a decrease of 0.26 per cent over the previous year. At the end of 2011 the bank had 155 domestic branches and 2,637 outlets in more than 173 major cities in mainland China. The bank also had 12 overseas branches in Hong Kong, New York, Tokyo, Singapore, Seoul, Frankfurt, Macau, Ho Chi Minh City, Sydney, and San Francisco. Furthermore, it also had an outlet in the UK – Bank of Communication (UK) Co. Ltd – and a representative office in Taipei.

Joint stock commercial banks

There are 12 joint stock commercial banks (JSCBs) at the moment in China: CITIC Bank, Industrial Bank, China Merchants Bank, Shanghai Pudong Development Bank, Huaxia Bank, China Minsheng Bank, Shenzhen Development Bank (Ping An Bank), China Everbright Bank, Guangdong Development Bank (Guangfa Bank), Evergrowing Bank, China Zheshang Bank, and Bohai Bank. According to the

2011 annual statement from the China Banking Regulatory Commission (CBRC), the total assets of JSCBs were RMB18.38 trillion at the end of 2011, accounting for 16.22 per cent of total assets in the Chinese banking sector, which was 0.58 per cent higher than 2010. JSCBs are allowed to engage in a wide range of banking services such as accepting deposits, extending loans, and providing foreign exchange and international transaction services. Rather than making loans to large enterprises, JSCBs mainly provide credit to small and medium-size enterprises (SMEs). For the sake of external monitoring and thereby improving bank management, all JSCBs are encouraged to get themselves listed on stock exchanges. In the footsteps of Shenzhen Development Bank (Ping An Bank), which made its IPO in 1997, seven other JSCBs are listed on stock exchanges including Industrial Bank, China Everbright Bank, China Merchants Bank, Shanghai Pudong Development Bank, Huaxia Bank, China CITIC Bank, and China Minsheng Bank. The after-tax profit of JSCBs at the end of 2011 was RMB200.5 billion, a growth rate of 47.6 per cent over the previous year.

Policy banks

The policy-lending obligations undertaken by the Big 4 state-owned commercial banks (SOCBs) were taken over by the three policy banks that were established in 1994. Each of the three policy banks is responsible for providing credit to different sectors of the economy. The Agricultural Development Bank of China (ADBC) mainly promotes the development of agriculture and rural areas by: (1) raising funds for agricultural policy businesses in accordance with laws, regulations, and policies; (2) undertaking agriculture policy credit business as specified by the central government and agriculture-related commercial business approved by the regulators; (3) serving as an agent of the state treasury by allocating special funds supporting agriculture. The China Development Bank (CDB) supports the development of national infrastructure, basic industry, key emerging sectors, and national priority projects; promotes coordinated regional development and urbanization by financing small business, education, healthcare, agricultural/rural investment, low-income housing, and environmental initiatives; facilitates China's cross-border investment and global business cooperation. The Export–Import Bank of China (EXIM) facilitates the export and import of Chinese mechanical and electronic products, and new and high-tech products; assists Chinese companies with comparative advantage in their offshore contract projects and outbound investment; and promotes Sino-foreign relationships and international economic and trade cooperation. The total assets of the three policy banks at the end of 2011 were RMB9.31 trillion, a growth rate of 21.7 per cent over 2010, while the after-tax profit of the policy banks at the end of 2011 was RMB53.67 billion, a growth rate of 29.3 per cent over 2010.

City commercial banks

City commercial banks (CCBs) are the result of reconstructing and consolidating urban credit cooperatives (UCCs) since the mid-1990s. Althought characterized as being small size in terms of total assets, by the end of 2011 there were 144 of them with total assets of RMB9.98 trillion, accounting for 8.8 per cent of total banking institution assets in China, which represented a growth rate of 0.6 per cent over the previous year. The ownership of CCBs is made up of local governments and urban enterprises with the former holding substantially larger shares. Thus, local government has direct control over the operation of CCBs, and the CCBs themselves have little power in terms of allocating credit and making lending decisions. Strong intervention from local government has led to the buildup of non-performing loans in CCBs.

The business scope of CCBs was limited to its home city. Unlike JSCBs, CCBs were not allowed to operate at the national or regional level and thus they were prevented from potential expansion. However, the limitations on the business scope of CCBs was gradually being relaxed by the regulatory authorities. Those CCBs that were well managed and had performed well are allowed to engage in business in other cities. The first city commercial bank to get such approval was the Bank of Shanghai, which opened a branch in Ningbo in 2005. Because of unequal economic development among different cities, the trans-regional operations of CCBs reduced economic fluctuations in bank performance to a minimum and at the same time increased the competitive power of CCBs. In order to promote diversification of investment, accelerate the improvement of corporate governance structure, and increase the capital adequacy ratio, foreign strategic investment started in Chinese banking sector in 2001, when an international financial corporation took 7 per cent of the stake in the Bank of Shanghai. Until the end of 2008, 11 CCBs had opened up to foreign strategic investors.[6]

Overview of the Chinese banking sector from 2003 to 2011

Figure 2.1 shows the total assets of the Chinese banking sector over the period 2003 to 2011. The figure shows the assets of the Chinese banking sector constantly increased and reached the

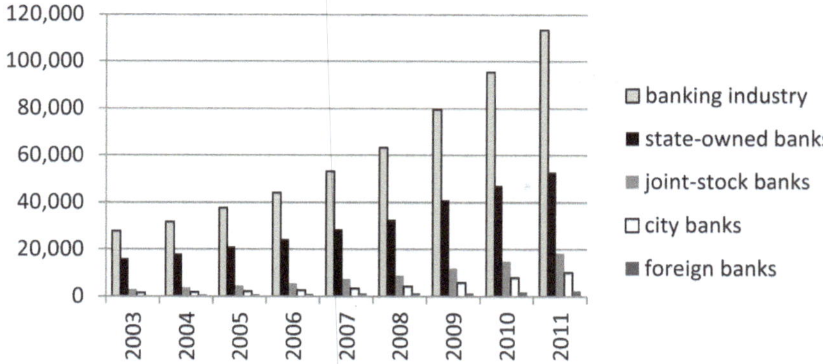

Figure 2.1 **Total assets of Chinese banking sector over 2003–11 (RMB billion)**

Source: CBRC.

highest point in 2011, when the value reached RMB113.29 trillion. This growth of assets in the banking sector suggests that there was relatively higher demand for banking services in China, this growth being attributed to GDP growth in China over the examined period. The figure also shows the total assets of different ownerships of Chinese banks (SOCBs, JSCBs, CCBs, and foreign banks). It can be seen that the assets of all groups of commercial banks constantly increased up to 2011; this indicates that the different ownerships of Chinese banks had undergone much development over the examined period.

Figure 2.2 shows the market share of total assets for different ownerships of Chinese commercial banks. The market share of total assets of SOCBs, which have dominated the Chinese banking sector for a long time, constantly declined over the examined period reaching the lowest point in 2011 when the assets of SOCBs accounted for 46.46 per cent of total banking sector assets. By contrast, the market share of JSCBs and CCBs in China constantly increased. This figure shows that, although Chinese state-owned commercial banks are the biggest banking

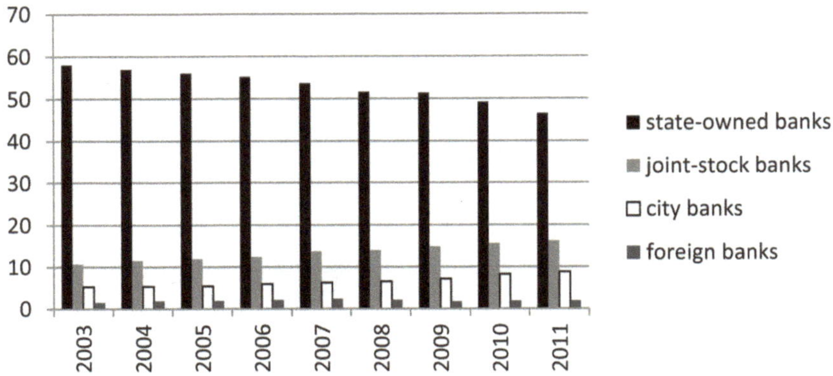

Figure 2.2 **Market share of state-owned, joint stock, city, and foreign banks in total banking sector assets over 2003–11 (%)**

Source: CBRC.

group in China, their market power decreased slightly as competition in the Chinese banking sector grew. The figure further shows that the market share of foreign banks in China constantly increased from 2003 until 2008 when a slight decrease can be seen. The increasing market share of foreign banks in China was attributed to China gradually opening up its banking sector after its entry to the WTO at the end of 2001, as discussed in the "China's banking reforms" section. By the end of 2006, foreign banks were treated exactly the same as domestic banks which resulted in foreign banks increasing the volume of their business and led to an increase in their market share.

Figure 2.3 shows the volume of non-performing loans in the Chinese banking sector during the period 2003–11 in terms of the banking sector as a whole. It can be seen that the volume of non-performing loans constantly declined over the period 2003–06, whereas there is a slight increase in 2007. The pattern shown by SOCBs follows that of the whole banking sector in that the volume of non-performing loans constantly decreased until 2007 when there was a slight increase in the volume of non-

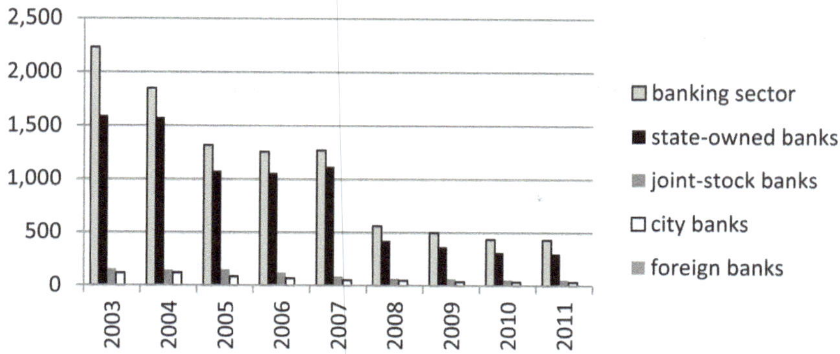

Figure 2.3 **Volume of non-performing loans in Chinese banking sector over 2003–11 (RMB billion)**

Source: CBRC.

performing loans. A reasonable conclusion was that the increasing volume of non-performing loans in the Chinese banking sector in 2007 can be attributed to the increasing volume of non-performing loans in SOCBs. Whereas the reason for the increasing volume of non-performing loans in SOCBs in 2007 can be explained by the fact that by the end of 2006 there was no restriction on foreign banks engaging in business and there were no geographic restrictions. In other words, foreign banks could offer banking services throughout China and were treated exactly the same as domestic banks. As SOCBs have branches all over the country, the increased competition between state-owned and foreign banks resulted in SOCBs taking higher risks, thus leading to an increase in the volume of non-performing loans. Compared with an increase in the volume of non-performing loans in SOCBs, there was a slight decrease in the volume of non-performing loans in foreign banks; this can be attributed to the greater experience foreign banks had of risk management. The figure further shows that there was a dramatic decrease in the volume of non-performing loans in 2008 for SOCBs; this can be attributed to the Olympic Games held by Beijing in the same year, which not only stimulated investment but further reduced the default rate leading to a decline in the volume of non-performing loans. The figure also shows that rather than experiencing a decline in the volume of non-performing loans, the foreign banks in China saw an increase in the volume of non-performing loans; this can possibly be explained by the fact that the 2008 Olympic Games attracted more foreign banks to enter the Chinese market. The increased competition among foreign banks made them take higher risks and hence an increase in the volume of non-performing loans. Figure 2.3 clearly shows that the volume of non-performing loans in SOCBs was substantially higher than in JSCBs and CCBs. There were a couple of reasons for this finding: first, SOCBs normally made loans to SOEs; the poor performance of SOEs increased the default rate and led to an increase in the volume of non-performing loans. Second, as was indicative of Chinese banking reform, the Chinese government provided different schemes to write off the non-performing loans of state-owned banks such as capital injection and the use of asset management companies, which had the effect of making managers in state-owned banks less careful when it came to credit monitoring. Once again the likely outcome was an increase in the volume of non-performing loans.

Figure 2.4 shows the non-performing loan ratio of the Chinese banking sector over the period 2003–11. The figure shows that the banking sector in China as a whole experienced a decrease in the non-performing loan ratio over the period. The same pattern can be seen for SOCBs, JSCBs, and CCBs. As far as SOCBs are concerned, the figure shows that the non-performing loan ratios dropped dramatically in 2005 and 2008. The substantial decrease in the non-performing loan ratio in 2005 can be attributed to non-performing loans being written off by the asset management companies allocated to state-owned banks; whereas the dramatic decline in the non-performing

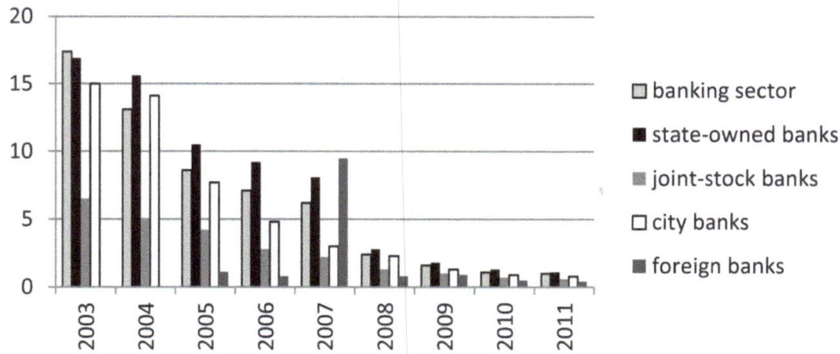

Figure 2.4 **Non-performing loan ratios in Chinese banking sector over 2003–11**

Source: CBRC.

loan ratio in 2008 can be explained by the Olympic Games being held, which improved the quality of bank lending. Unlike the volume of non-performing loans reflected in Figure 2.3, which shows CCBs had a lower volume of non-performing loans than SOCBs and JSCBs, Figure 2.4 suggests that JSCBs had a lower non-performing loan ratio than SOCBs and CCBs. This finding can be explained by SOCBs and CCBs being controlled by central and local government and having less freedom in credit allocation, whereas the main shareholders of JSCBs included SOEs and foreign banks. The advanced technology used for risk management together with more freedom and rational credit allocation led to a lower non-performing loan ratio.

The decline in non-performing loans in the Chinese banking sector coincided with the improvement in capital adequacy of commercial banks. Table 2.1 shows that, as of the end of 2003, only eight commercial banks, which accounted for less than 1 per cent of banking system assets, had achieved the minimum capital adequacy ratio of 8 per cent set by the Bank for International Settlements (BIS). As discussed in the "China's banking reforms" section, by the end of 2006 all commercial

Table 2.1 Progress in meeting capital adequacy

	2003	2004	2005	2006	2007	2008	2009
Number of banks meeting minimum capital adequacy requirement	8	30	53	100	161	204	239
Share of total banking system assets (%)	0.6	47.5	75.1	77.4	79	99.9	100

Source: CBRC.

banks were required to hold a capital adequacy ratio of 8 per cent. However, this target was not achieved because, as the table indicates, by the end of 2006 only 100 banks accounting for 77.4 per cent of total banking sector assets had achieved the goal. However, by the end of 2009 all commercial banks had met the goal of holding the minimum capital adequacy ratio set by the BIS. More specifically, four SOCBs – the China Construction Bank, Industrial and Commercial Bank of China, Bank of China, and Bank of Communication – had a capital adequacy ratio of more than 11 per cent, while the average capital adequacy ratio of all listed commercial banks was 8.8 per cent.

Table 2.2 shows the pre-tax profit of commercial banks in the Chinese banking sector over the period 2003–11. It can be seen that the banking sector as a whole experienced an increase in bank profitability over the period. The same situation applied to all different ownerships of commercial banks. However, it can clearly be seen that the profitability of SOCBs in 2003 was −3.2, which can be explained by the large volume of non-performing loans, whereas there was a dramatic increase in the profitability of SOCBs in 2004 and 2005; this can largely be attributed to a couple of major non-performing loan write-offs undertaken by

Table 2.2 Pre-tax profit of commercial banks (RMB Billion)

	2003	2004	2005	2006	2007*	2008*	2009*	2010*	2011*
Banking sector	28.5	98.5	247	325	413.4	554.9	668.4	899.09	1,251.87
State-owned banks	–3.2	45.9	156.1	197.5	246.6	354.2	400.1	515.12	664.66
Joint-stock banks	14.7	17.6	28.9	43.4	56.4	84.1	92.5	135.8	200.5
City banks	5.4	8.7	12.1	18.1	24.8	40.8	49.7	76.98	108.09
Foreign banks	1.7	2.4	3.7	5.8	6.1	11.9	6.45	7.78	16.73

* After tax profit
Source: CBRC.

four asset management companies in 2004 and 2005 and an injection of capital to state-owned banks in 2004 and 2005 by the Chinese government. The table shows that all ownerships of commercial banks experienced a slightly higher increase in profitability in 2008 as a result of the Olympic Games being held in China.

Summary and conclusion

This chapter begins by reviewing Chinese banking reforms since 1979 and then gives a brief introduction to the structure of the Chinese banking sector including banking regulatory authorities and different ownerships of Chinese financial institutions. The chapter also overviews the development of the Chinese banking sector between 2003 and 2011; this section focuses on different banking indicators such as banking sector assets, the banking capital adequacy ratio, banking profitability, and non-performing loans in the Chinese banking sector. More importantly, the abovementioned indicators are analysed by ownership types (i.e., SOCBs, JSCBs, CCBs, and foreign banks). The indicators are explained and clearly linked to relevant policies initiated by the Chinese government.

In conclusion, it is argued that China's banking reforms succeeded in creating a competitive environment, reducing the volume of non-performing loans and increasing profitability in the Chinese banking sector. For instance, by removing restrictions on foreign banks engaging in business in China helped the Chinese banking sector create a more competitive environment. Moreover, by establishing four asset management companies and by making capital injections the Chinese government substantially reduced the volume of non-performing loans in Chinese state-owned banks and further increased their profitability. Although the first target regarding the capital adequacy ratio of 8 per cent set by the Chinese government was not achieved by the end of 2006, all commercial banks met the requirement by the end of 2009. What is more, four SOCBs held a capital adequacy ratio of 11 per cent, while the average capital adequacy ratio of 14 listed commercial banks was 8.8 per cent, which was higher than the 8 per cent set by the BIS.

After several rounds of banking reforms, China's banking sector seemed to have become more competitive, as evidenced by the market share of SOCBs constantly decreasing over the period 2003–2011 although the rate of decrease was very small. The market share of JSCBs and CCBs, on the other hand, constantly increased over the period. It can be seen that SOCBs at the end of 2011 held nearly 50 per cent of total banking sector assets which indicates that SOCBs still dominated in the Chinese banking system. It can also be seen that the non-performing loan ratio in the Chinese banking sector constantly decreased over the period 2003–11. Nevertheless, SOCBs still had a substantially higher volume of non-performing loans and a higher non-performing loan ratio than JSCBs and CCBs. The higher volume of non-performing loans in the Chinese banking sector can be attributed to loans made by Chinese commercial banks being largely concentrated in the state-owned sector. Chinese commercial banks should be encouraged to increase the amounts of credit allocated to SMEs because these types of enterprises are an important part of the country's economy. Subject to credit checks and risk monitoring, the allocation of credit to these enterprises has the added advantage of helping Chinese commercial banks reduce the volume of non-performing loans and the non-performing loan ratio.

As far as research into the Chinese banking industry goes, apart from bank profitability, there have been a number of investigations into the efficiency of the Chinese banking sector, another important aspect of bank performance. Most studies show that JSCBs are the most efficient whereas SOCBs are the least (see Chapter 4 for details). This book builds on previous research in the Chinese banking by (1) investigating comprehensive aspects of bank performance in China including bank profitability, efficiency, and productivity; (2) using different indicators to look at the risk-taking behaviour of the Chinese banking sector such as the ratio of loan loss provisions to total loans, the Z-score and stability inefficiency, the impact of risk on bank performance, and the effect of competition on the risk-taking behavior of Chinese banks will also be examined. (3) It is the first book to use both non-structural indicators (Lerner index and Panzar–Rosse H statistic) and a structural indicator (three-bank concentration ratio) to examine the competitive condition in the Chinese banking industry. It is also the first book to examine the relationship between risk and performance in the Chinese banking industry.

Notes

1. In 2006 the PBC included it as a state-owned commercial banks. Therefore, it became the fifth state-owned commercial banks after the CCB, ABC, ICBC, and BOC.
2. On 14 June 2012 the Shenzhen Development Bank merged with and was acquired by Ping An Bank. As a result of the M&A its new name is Ping An Bank.
3. On 8 April 2011 the name of the Guangdong Development Bank was changed to China Guangfa Bank after official approval from the China Banking Regulatory Commission and the relevant government department.
4. The four state-owned commercial banks are the China Construction Bank, Bank of China, Industrial and Commercial Bank of China and the Bank of Communication.

5. The nine JSCBs are the Shanghai Pudong Development Bank, China Industrial Bank, Shenzhen Development Bank, Minsheng Bank, Hua Xia Bank, China Citic Bank, Guangdong Development Bank, Evergrowing Bank and Bohai Bank.
6. The 11 CCBs are the Bank of Shanghai, Xi An city commercial bank, Qilu Bank, Bank of Beijing, Bank of Hangzhou, Nanchong Commercial Bank, Bank of Nanjing, Bank of Tianjin, Bank of Ningbo, Bank of Chongqing and Bank of Qingdao.

3

Corporate governance in the banking sector

Abstract: Corporate governance is an important topic in all kinds of companies and has attracted attention from government, company directors, stakeholders, and academic researchers. Appropriate development of the relationship between company and different stakeholders, which is addressed by corporate governance, is supposed to promote improvements in firm performance. Banks, as important financial institutions, play important roles in a country's economy. They deal with the relationship between management and different shareholders as well as depositors. There are different interpretations of the meaning of corporate governance.

The chapter begins by defining corporate governance. This is followed by a section entitled "Theories relevant to corporate governance". There then follow sections entitled "Corporate governance problems of banks" and "Bank corporate governance in practice". The chapter ends with a conclusion.

Key words: definition of corporate governance, theories of corporate governance, corporate governance problems, corporate governance in practice.

Definition of corporate governance

Corporate governance is a hot issue discussed by a wide range of interested parties including government officials, company managers, and even academic researchers because of its importance to the economic growth of a corporation and society as a whole. However, there is no consensus on its definition. Scholars from different fields define it differently, but a single version of the definition has not been accepted by the public at large.

Blair (1995) argues that corporate governance has to do with the structure and functioning of boards of directors. Donaldson (1990) states that corporate governance is the structure under which the highest level of management within an organization is controlled by the board of directors, associated structures, executive incentives, and other monitoring and bonding schemes. Tricker (1994) argues that a boardroom should broadly include the owners and all those interested in the affairs of a company such as creditors, debt financiers, analysts, auditors, and corporate regulators.

Corporate governance can be regarded as a range of arrangements within a corporation which clearly identify the relationship between shareholders and managers of the corporation. Shleifer and Vishny (1997) suggest that the specific structure of corporate governance represents the way in which those who fund the corporation can ensure they will get a return on their investment. Monks and Minow (1995) argue that corporate governance is the relationship between an organization's different participants, which impacts the direction and performance of the corporation. A corporation's principal participants are the stakeholders, the management, and the board of directors.

Corporate governance can be defined in a narrow sense as above. Some scholars define it in a much broader way. Keasey and Wright (1993) argue that corporate governance is the structure, process, culture, and systems that are closely related to successful operation of an organization. CC (1992) posits that corporate governance seeks to find a balance between economic and social goals, and at the same time represents a balance between the achievement of individual and communal goals. The purpose of corporate governance is to make sure that resources are used as efficiently as possible, that the stewardship of these resources is accountable, and that the interests of individuals, corporations, and society are aligned as closely as possible.

The most widely accepted definition of corporate governance is provided by the OECD (1999). It argues that corporate governance represents a system or structure that offers guidelines to direct and control business operations. The rights and responsibilities of different participants within the corporation including the board, managers, and stakeholders are clearly identified. Furthermore, rules and procedures are specified that need to be followed when making decisions on corporate affairs. Thus, corporate governance is a structure that incorporates the objectives of the corporation, the methods to achieve the objectives, and ways of monitoring the performance of the corporation.

The World Bank defines corporate governance from two different standpoints (WB, 1999): in the context of a corporation, corporate governance concerns maintaining a good relationship between the owners, management, and various stakeholders such as employees, customers, suppliers, and investors. In particular, special attention is paid to the board of directors, their ability to obtain long-term value for the corporation, and balance the interests among the different parties. In the context of public policy (the second standpoint), corporate governance focusses on two issues: (1) a company's survival, growth, and development; and (2) accountability regarding the exercise of power and control over companies.

Many economic and social issues are covered by corporate governance, and the subject is expanding across different disciplines such as economy, finance, law, sociology, politics, and organizational theory. Different scholars with different areas of expertise have different views on the concept of corporate governance. However, the fundamental question that needs to be addressed relates to corporate power and wealth and how they should be controlled. The following section explains a number of schools of thought that are relevant to corporate governance.

Theories relevant to corporate governance

Corporate governance has developed alongside the theory of the firm. Controversy reigns regarding the reasons firms exist and the rationale behind controlling the firm, issues that have aroused a lot of interest from the general public. According to Smith (1976), in the eighteenth century the issue of "negligence and profusion" often cropped up when managers handled "other people's money" in joint stock companies. As time went by, the fundamental explanation of the relationship between investor and corporation became clear (Berle and Means, 1932). They argue that the development of a market and a country would separate the ownership and control of a public corporation into two parts. The main problem in corporate governance, indeed, relates to the separation between ownership and control. Some corporate control theories aim to address this issue. The following subsections discuss the three schools of thought on corporate governance: agency theory, stakeholder theory, and stewardship theory.

Agency theory

The agency theory of corporate governance was put forward by Alchian and Demsetz (1972) and Jensen and Meckling (1976). They argued that firms can be regarded as a nexus for a set of contracting relationships among individuals, whereas classical economics regards firms as single-product entities with the purpose of maximizing profit. Learmount (2004) suggests that firms can be explained as contracts that are repeatedly negotiated by different individuals wishing to maximize their own profit.

Agency theory explains the behaviour of a firm from the perspectives of various contracts between different parties. Shareholders who contribute funds for a firm to operate are not regarded as the owners of the firms; they are the risk takers of the firm. In the real world the managers of firms obtain funds from investors who believe the managers have the ability to use the funds efficiently and effectively to generate profits for the firms. The managers sign contracts that identify the activities they should engage in and specify the way in which profit is allocated between managers and investors. Since it is very difficult to describe and forecast future contingencies, the contracts signed by managers are difficult to implement (Shbeifer and Vishny, 1997). Consequently, managers obtain the right to make decisions that go beyond what is stipulated in their contracts. It is human nature to make decisions that suit an individual's own interests; it is no different for managers. They will make decisions that are beneficial for themselves and have scant regard for shareholders' interests. This brings about the principal's problem (Ross, 1973) and the agency problem (Fama and Jensen 1983a, b).

Agency theory describes managers as agents and shareholders as principals. The theory argues that the value of a firm cannot be maximized if appropriate incentives or adequate monitoring are not effective enough to restrain firm managers from using their own discretion to maximize their own benefits. This can be further explained when looked at like this: first, the interests of principals and agents need to be matched to overcome their different preferences regarding firm activity and different attitudes towards risk exposure. Second, since information asymmetry argues that the principal and agent hold different amounts of information (normally the agent has access to more information than the principal), it is difficult and expensive for the principal to monitor the agent's behaviour. Jensen and Meckling (1976) identify three agency costs for principals to monitor agent behaviour: monitoring management, binding the agent to the principal, and residual losses.

Fligstein and Freeland (1995) argue that the most efficient contract used to govern the principal–agent relationship is determined by agency theory. The establishment of this contract is also the focus of agency theory. A number of issues should be included and clearly specified in the contract such as agent duties, rewards, and the rights of the principal to monitor the agent's performance. The behaviour-oriented contract and the outcome-oriented contract are the two main contracts put in place. The behaviour-oriented contract focusses on using salaries as the main rewards to the agent while various different rewards are given to the agent under outcome-oriented contracts such as commission, stock options, and transfer of property rights. The choice between which of these contracts to use to reward the agent is crucial and key to solution of the agency problem.

Agency theory played an important role in understanding corporate governance in the twentieth century. It contributed significantly to understanding the mechanism involved in the working of firms. Perrow (1986) argues that the importance of incentives and the self-interest in organizational thinking were re-established by agency theory. Furthermore, Eisenhardt (1989) suggests that the main contribution of agency theory lies in the fact that it identifies how to treat information and risk in the operation of a firm. On the other hand, there are quite a few limitations to agency theory. It makes the assumption that human beings are "individualistic" and "self-interested". However, Doucouliagos (1994) states that this assumption is not in line with the nature of complexity of human action. Moran and Ghoshal (1996) argue that the assumption made by this theory has a significant and negative impact on human behaviour. In other words, the assumption of this theory encourages human beings to be individualistic and self-interested.

Furthermore, agency theory simplifies a firm by confining its participants to two groups: managers and shareholders. The operation of a firm clearly needs to consider the impact of its behaviour on different groups of stakeholders. On the one hand, equity investment can be attracted and retained by a firm that is accountable to its shareholders; on the other hand, the interests of other groups of stakeholders also need to be given proper consideration. Eisenhardt (1989) argues that a partial view of the world is represented by agency theory because it ignores much of the complexity of a firm.

Stakeholder theory

Many scholars have helped develop the stakeholder concept (see Clark, 1916; Dodd, 1932; and Berle and Means, 1932). A new way of thinking about business organization was initiated by Freeman (1984). He not only explains the relationship between the firm itself and the external environment, but also the relationship between the behaviour of a firm and the environment, which provides the basis for stakeholder theory. Stakeholder theory was also defined by Clarkson (1994), who argues that a firm is made up of stakeholders and operates within society, which sets up the necessary legal and market infrastructure for the activities of a firm. He further argues that value or wealth creation for stakeholders is the main purpose of firms.

The way in which control is exercised within firms is

determined by the entire network of informal and formal relations, which is the focus of stakeholder theory. Different relations also affect the way in which risk and return are allocated among different stakeholders. Freeman (1984) argues that stakeholders comprise individuals and entities that can be influenced or can affect achievement of the objectives of a firm. Stakeholders are mainly classified into two groups: primary stakeholders and secondary stakeholders. Primary stakeholders mainly include those who are directly affected by a company's activities such as shareholders, creditors, customers, suppliers, managers and employees, and state and local communities. Secondary stakeholders are those who are not directly and obviously influenced by a company's success or failure. This group of stakeholders includes regulators, competitors, media, and civic institutions.

Donaldson and Preston (1995) argue that stakeholder theory can be broken down into three types: descriptive, instrumental, and normative. Stakeholder theory can be descriptive because specific corporate characteristics and behaviours can be described and explained. Stakeholder theory can be instrumental because the relationship between stakeholder management and the achievement of the objectives of a firm can be identified. Stakeholder theory can be normative because the function of a firm can be interpreted and moral and philosophical guidelines in the operation of a firm can be identified.

As discussed above, stakeholder theory can be divided into three types, which can be explained as follows. Instrumental theory is that part of stakeholder theory that emphasizes the value of stakeholders because of the positive impact they are believed to have on efficiency, profitability, competition, and economic success. Normative theory, on the other hand, focusses on the intrinsic value of the interests of stakeholders.

Normative theory argues that firms should conform to normative and moral commitments in order to maintain a good managerial relationship with stakeholders and ensure stakeholders are not purely and solely treated and used to maximize profits. It is pivotal for firms to abide by certain moral principles that provide guidance concerning the way business is conducted and the way stakeholders are treated (Campbell, 1977).

Stakeholder theory can be explained from a number of different perspectives. It can be interpreted from a normative perspective, which is attributed to the framework of normative stakeholder theory put forward by Donaldson and Preston (1995). It can be interpreted from a practical perspective Jones (1995). He argues that a genuine commitment to ethical principles contributes to the instrumental benefit of stakeholders. Mutual trust and cooperation in stakeholder relationships play important roles in creating competitive advantages for firms. Clarkson (1995) argues that when the framework within which a corporation's relationship with its stakeholders is managed in accordance with normative theory, it can analyse and evaluate such concepts as corporate social responsibility, corporate social responsiveness, and corporate social performance more effectively. These may explain, at least to a certain extent, the reason stakeholder theory provides a basic and vital background to corporate strategy, economics, public policy, and business ethics.

The development of stakeholder theory largely depends on economic theory. Stakeholder theory agrees with agency theory to the extent that firms mainly deal with various contracts among different parties and both identify managers as agents. The difference between agency theory and stakeholder theory lies in the former focussing on legal and implied contracts in the principal–agent relationship while the latter includes a social/moral contract as well. Both implicit and explicit contractual relationships were noted by Hill and Jones (1992) when they further developed stakeholder–agency theory.

Stakeholder theory has a number of limitations. For instance, it does not provide any guidance when it comes to management decision making. Friedman and Miles (2002) argue that the boundary among stakeholder groups is clearly defined by stakeholder theory. However, in the real world there is diversity regarding stakeholder interests. Furthermore, there are diverse and conflicting interests between different groups of stakeholders and even within a single group of stakeholders. Since management has responsibilities towards different groups of stakeholders, stakeholder theory is not clear when it comes to balancing such interests between different groups of stakeholders.

Stewardship theory

The stewardship theory of corporate governance argues that the manager of a firm is the steward of the firm's assets rather than the agent of the shareholders (Donaldson and Davis, 1991; Davis et al., 1997). This theory further argues that there are two different behaviours taken by firm managers: collectivistic and individualistic. The former is supposed to have higher utility than the latter.

Stewardship theory suggests that a firm can be run efficiently if four important requirements are met: depth of knowledge, commitment, access to current operating information, and technical expertise. According to this viewpoint, governance structures and mechanisms should be empowered by directors, the purpose of which is to maximize the benefit of a steward.

Donaldson and Davis (1991) argue that a firm's corporate governance structure is closely linked to actions of its CEO. More specifically, if a firm's corporate governance structure gives the CEO a lot of authority and discretion, it will facilitate the CEO engaging in pro-organizational behaviors.

Stewardship theory also demonstrates the close relationship between the role of the director and firm performance, arguing that manager behaviour is collective and hence helpful to attaining the objectives of the organization. In other words, collective behaviour leads to growth in sales and higher profitability. The collective behaviour of managers will also benefit principals such as shareholders in terms of its positive influence on share price and dividends. Stewardship theory makes the assumption that the success of the organization is closely linked to principal satisfaction. The theory further argues that improved firm performance and the resultant increased shareholder wealth maximize the utility functions of managers. Hence, there is a relationship between directors, managers, and firm performance. Directors empower managers and managers are responsible for improving firm performance.

The empirical literature comes up with different findings regarding stewardship theory. Some studies find that stewardship theory's executive-chaired boards significantly contribute to improving corporate performance (Donaldson and Davis, 1991; Finkelstein and D'Aveni, 1994), while other studies suggest that executive-chaired and outsider-chaired boards are not clearly related to firm performance (Chaganti et al., 1985; Molz, 1988). The relationship between executive/outsider-chaired boards and corporate performance needs to be validated by further research because of the newness of stewardship theory (Davis et al., 1997).

Corporate governance problems of banks

It is well known that every firm is affected by the principal–agent problem between managers and shareholders. Macey and O'Hara (2003) argue that the agency problem in banks is very serious. This section discusses the corporate governance problems of banks from four different perspectives: corporate governance structure, government safety nets, opaqueness, and market competition.

Corporate governance structure

Many parties have an interest in the activities of a bank including shareholders, depositors, and employers. Different parties make the governance of banking institutions complicated. Heffernan (1996) points out that banks engage in the business of asset management, while the source of funds to support assets is mainly made up of deposits and other liabilities. Deposits account for a large proportion of a bank's liabilities, they provide the funds to make loans, and they are also available to depositors to withdraw on demand.

Furthermore, the balance sheet of a bank is substantially different from that of other firms because of the specific nature of banking. On the one hand, banks have a higher debt–equity ratio than other kinds of firms because funds in the banking business are mostly made up of deposits. On the other hand, in the traditional loan–deposit business engaged in by banks there is a mismatch between the liquidity of liabilities and assets. In other words, banks have liabilities (deposits) that are highly liquid while assets (loans) are relatively less liquid. Therefore, banks need to inspire more confidence in depositors for them to keep their funds in banks for longer terms, while external shocks to the banking sector will have the opposite effect and encourage them to withdraw their money from the banks. The loans made by banks cannot be claimed back immediately to meet the demand from depositors – the result would be bankruptcy. Thus, government regulation plays an important role in banking.

All risks to the banking sector are paid great attention by governments. The stability of the banking sector is known to contribute to the stability of the financial sector and economic growth as well, whereas instability in the banking sector has a significant and negative impact on the economy as a whole. For instance, a bank that is not managed very well runs the risk of a bank run or collapse, a bank that goes bankrupt will decrease the funds available to other sectors of the economy, and the resultant deterioration in public confidence will lead to the collapse of solvent banks too (Diamond and Dybvig, 1983). The contagion effect in the banking sector is particularly serious compared with other economic sectors, and significantly and negatively influences the whole economy. Thus, governments pay great attention to the stability of the banking sector. They have different ways of supporting the banking sector and promoting bank stability such as regulations, deposit insurance, and government ownership of banks.

In addition to governments, rating agencies are closely linked with banks. Rating agencies provide information about the stability of banks, considered to be an alternative source of information to the financial statement of a bank. Apart from information related to the risk/stability of banks, rating agencies also provide information regarding the strengths and weaknesses of banks, which plays an important role in influencing the corporate governance of banks. The influence can be explained from the internal stakeholder perspective and the external stakeholder perspective. For internal stakeholders like managements and boards the information provided by rating agencies can be regarded as a signal for the bank to take measures to improve their operations, while for external stakeholders like investors and depositors the information reveals the creditworthiness of the bank. It also helps the regulator come up with relevant policies on capital requirements and investment.

Government safety nets

Most countries around the world have financial safety nets provided by their governments such as explicit deposit insurance schemes or implicit deposit protection guarantees. A further safety net is offered by the government in the form of bank regulation and supervision. The purpose of government safety nets is to decrease the degree of contagion from insolvent banks to solvent banks and reduce the possibility of financial system breakdowns. Government safety nets also help to reduce bankruptcy costs or other costs incurred as a result of financial instability. However, the incentives of private stakeholders to monitor banks are lessened because of the existence of such safety nets.

Garten (1986) argues that bank depositors are very well positioned to impose discipline on bank management. Bank deposits are the main source of funds for banks to keep operating. Furthermore, depositors pay a great deal of attention to the possibility of a bank run and quickly respond to different types of bank risk. Demirguc-Kunt and Huizinga (1999a) and Berger (1991) suggest that when the cost of bank operation increases and banks face more uncertainty, depositors normally react in one of two ways: either requiring a higher return for their deposits or withdrawing their deposits from the bank. Explicit government deposit insurance schemes and implicit guarantees such as the "too big to fail" issue actually have a negative impact on the incentives of depositors to monitor bank risk. More specifically, Rochet (1992) and Blum (2002) indicate that, absent the corporate governance problem between shareholders and bank managers, uninsured bank deposits will induce bank managers to undertake risk behaviour more efficiently and rationally. This can be explained by the fact that the higher risk-taking behaviour undertaken by bank managers will increase the demand for higher returns or compensation from depositors. In this sense there is no moral hazard issue. On the other hand, insured bank deposits will induce bank managers to undertake risk less rationally and less efficiently and depositors will bear the brunt of this less-than-rational risk-taking behaviour because the returns required by depositors do not increase even when banks take higher risks. In this sense there is a moral hazard issue regarding the choice of risk made by banks.

Government deposit protection guarantees are also associated with the moral hazard issue in banks. As a result of the "too big to fail" issue, the amount of deposits attracted by a bank is not a good indicator of the risk condition of that bank's asset profile. Government deposit protection guarantees will also reduce the incentive for bank managers to improve bank performance. Furthermore, banks are reluctant to make efforts to improve corporate governance because all the deposits within the bank are insured and the depositors have little incentive to monitor the bank's operation. Therefore, banks normally take higher risk in their business operations because they consider higher risk means higher returns. Government deposit protection guarantees and the resultant moral hazard were at the root of the financial crisis to befall Western banking in the 1980s and Asia in 1997.

As mentioned earlier, financial safety is provided by governments through explicit insurance schemes and implicit deposit protection guarantees. Banking regulation and supervision, the third form of financial safety net offered by governments, are also associated with the moral hazard issue. Efficient and effective bank regulation and supervision can significantly reduce the moral hazard in banking.

Opaqueness

Caprio and Levine (2002) and Levine (2003) argue that information asymmetry and the agency problem are much more serious in the banking sector than in other sectors. Compared with non-financial institutions the activities of banks are much more opaque allowing them to hide their risk positions more easily. For example, banks allocate credit to firms that fail to pay back loans together with the interest by extending the loans for a longer period. In this way they can hide bad loans. Furthermore, the opacity of the banking business has been further muddied by a number of external environmental factors such as structural changes in the banking industry, globalization and resultant financial innovation, universal banking, and new technology. Therefore, the scope of a bank is hard to get to grips with and it is quite simply impossible for outsiders including bank supervisors to monitor the operation of a bank.

The corporate governance actions of private stakeholders are restricted in the face of such opaqueness. Baltensperger and Dermine (1987) argue that, of the various bank private stakeholders, depositors are affected the most by such opacity. They argue that depositors are inexperienced and have no information on the state in which the operation of a bank finds itself, and it is impossible for them to judge the quality of bank assets and the probability of an individual bank defaulting. Thus, bank managers have stronger incentives to pursue their own interests at the expense of those of other stakeholders.

Market competition

Most empirical literature argues that competition in the banking sector is weak. Prowse (1997) argues that manager behaviour is significantly affected by the degree of product market competition and the threat of takeover – something that seems to be stronger in non-banking institutions than banks. Product market competition and the threat of takeover are weakened in the banking sector because of opacity. The less intense product market competition that typifies the banking sector is attributed to banks wanting to establish long-run relationships with their customers in order to eliminate information problems. On the other hand, Caprio and Levine (2002) argue that the probability of takeover is low because of the shortage of information in the banking sector.

Bank corporate governance in practice

Ownership structure and governance

Unlike non-financial firms, there is ownership restriction in banking sectors worldwide (Barth et al., 2001). Ownership in the banking sector is restricted because it is considered to be closely related to such issues as the connection between the economic power of credit, conflicts of interest, and stability in the banking sector. In the banking sector a shareholder is only allowed to hold a certain number of shares in a bank and, should it exceed a certain level, the shareholder needs to obtain approval from the financial authorities. Ownership restriction has a major influence on the distribution of power between bank shareholders.

There has been a long history of government ownership of banks in both developing and developed countries. Although privatization has prevailed worldwide over the past two decades, state-owned institutions still control nearly 40 per cent of bank assets. There are two types of government ownership: dispersed ownership or concentrated ownership. On the one hand, state-owned banks have concentrated ownership if the government is viewed as a single entity. On the other hand, although government-owned banks are funded by money from the government as a whole, the actions of the banks are influenced by individuals within the government; when this is the case, state-owned banks are considered to have dispersed ownership.

There are many governance problems in state-owned banks because they are used by governments to support excessive government spending or to allocate credit to borrowers with a higher probability of loan default. Managers in state-owned banks have little incentive to perform their role properly for three main reasons: (1) strong political influence from government over the operation of a bank; (2) government officials push for credit to be allocated to sectors in which they have an interest, some of which may be less creditworthy; (3) the bank is operated under soft budget constraints. Furthermore, private stakeholders are less concerned about monitoring because they assume their credits are guaranteed. Caprio and Levine (2002) argue that government ownership reduces competition, increases the opacity of banking, and makes government supervision in the banking sector less effective.

In order to have a better understanding of the impact government ownership of banks has on corporate governance, it is worth pausing for a moment to examine the rationale behind government ownership of banks. Different theories/views explain the existence and role of state-owned banks from different perspectives. The next two paragraphs review two of them: the development view and the agency view.

The development view has its roots in the economic theory of institutions. The view is that privately owned banks play an important role in financial development and economic growth and that a proper investment system, such as that provided by government-owned banks, in an economy, should be provided by governments whose economic institutions are not developed enough. Gerschenkron (1962) supports the development view and further argues that government ownership of banks has a positive impact on the economic growth of underdeveloped countries. The difference between private banks and public sector banks lies in the latter being less concerned about maximizing profit, while putting more emphasis on maximizing broader social objectives. By contrast, private banks do not take social return into consideration. Stiglitz (1993) states that private banks do not focus their funds on supporting projects with higher social return and, further, that it is the responsibility of public financial institutions to solve the problem of market failure in the financial and credit market (Stiglitz and Weiss, 1981; Greenwald and Stiglitz, 1986). The development view is that government-owned banks promote economic development and improve general welfare at the same time. Park (1991) indicates that, when a banking system is dominated by state-owned banks, private non-bank financial companies can be affected by the government to perform in a socially desirable way and ensure their behaviour is in line with the development objectives of the country.

The agency view agrees with the development view to the extent that one of government's goals is to maximize social welfare. However, it further states that corruption and misallocation are possible by-products of the process (Banerjee, 1997; Hart et al., 1997). The agency view is in agreement with the development view in that market failure should be addressed by public financial institutions. Laffont and Tirole (1993) argue that low-powered incentives are not always bad because quality depends on them. By linking incentive problems to the control of state-owned enterprises (SOEs), the agency view is that the trade-off between internal and allocative efficiency is a factor determining the ultimate efficiency of SOEs (Tirole, 1994). This hypothesis further argues that, although state-owned banks focus their activities on socially profitable projects, less effort is exerted by managers in state-owned banks than those in private financial institutions. The agency view is that managers in state-owned banks work less hard and use resources for personal benefit such as career advancement, despite the achievement of social objectives being largely attributed to contributions made by state-owned banks than private banks.

Internal governance mechanism

Board of directors

The agency theory states that the board of directors is the primary internal control mechanism. The board of directors provides services to a firm's principals to monitor the behaviour of the managerial staff. Waldo (1985) and Fleischer et al. (1988) argue that the main tasks of a board of directors are: (1) monitoring managerial behaviour on behalf of the firm's owners; (2) formulating strategic decisions about firm activities; (3) detecting managerial misconduct and removing the relevant managers.

Macey and O'Hara (2003) argue that there are two duties that are incumbent on a firm's board of directors: duty of care and duty of loyalty. Even though banking institutions have the same responsibilities as non-banking firms, the boards of directors of banking institutions have additional responsibilities, which take the form of guidance, laws, and regulations. These extra responsibilities concern bank stability.

BCBS (1999) states that boards of directors in the banking sector play vital roles in creating good corporate governance. The corporate governance process involves: (1) setting up and enforcing clear lines of responsibility and accountability throughout the organization; (2) making sure that all members of the board are qualified and very clear on the role they undertake in corporate governance, and that they are free from interference from management or outsiders (special committees should be set up to look into risk management, auditing, financial compensation, and nomination); (3) making sure that financial compensation is in accordance with the ethical values, objectives, strategy, and control of the bank and that all managers and key personnel are motivated to work in the best interests of the bank; (4) making sure that corporate governance is conducted in a transparent way (more specifically, relevant information such as board management structures, organization structure, incentive structure, and transactions carried out by the bank should be disclosed to affiliates and related parties); (5) establishing strategic objectives, guiding corporate values, and preventing anything that could have a negative impact on the quality of corporate governance such as corruption, self-dealing, and giving favors to related parties; (6) making use of internal and external auditors effectively as an integral part of the control system.

Compensation of executives

An important corporate governance mechanism relates to the remuneration of senior management and other key personnel within banking institutions, the purpose of which is to align the interests of bank managers and shareholders. Compensation is given to bank executives and other managerial staff in order to increase their working incentives and efforts. Compensation takes and is based on a number of forms: (1) base salary, bonuses, new equity, and grants, etc; (2) capital gains on their portfolio of stocks and options; (3) assessment of their human capital by the markets which is reflected in their performance in their current jobs (Antle and Smith, 1986; Jensen and Murphy, 1990). Of these three main forms, the use of stock options to compensate bank executives has become controversial, as evidenced by the growing debate during recent years.

It is argued that agency problems can be significantly reduced through equity incentives and stock-based compensation because the underlying idea of this method is to connect CEO compensation and shareholder return. In other words, higher returns for shareholder leads to higher compensation for CEOs. This method motivates CEOs to make value-enhancing decisions in order to increase shareholders returns and thereby increase their own compensation. Houston and James (1995) find that banks whose CEOs hold large amounts of stock have a higher charter value. Furthermore, they suggest that the compensation bank CEOs receive does not necessarily lead to higher risk-taking behaviour. Becher et al. (2005) come up with similar findings in terms of US banks in the 1990s and conclude that stock-based compensation to bank CEOs can significantly contribute to the growth and development of the bank without increasing bank risk.

However, not all scholars agree with Houston and James (1995) and Becher et al. (2005). McConnell and Servaes (1990) argue that, once a certain level of managerial ownership is achieved, managers do not immerse themselves enough in their work; instead, they put their own benefit before that of other investors. Furthermore, Morck et al. (1988) and Short and Keasey (1999) argue that managerial entrenchment is rife in banks with higher levels of managerial ownership. Yermack (1995) and Aboody and Kasznik (2000) suggest that stock-based options induce bank managers to take greater risks. Managers have been known to manipulate the stock price fraudulently and in so doing increase the value of the stock and hence their own rewards.

Internal control

Internal control plays an important role in bank management. It is essential to the stability of banking institutions. Internal control is a process that involves all the people within the organization such as the board of directors, senior management and all levels of personnel. The system of internal control is not a policy or procedure implemented at a specific time, it is a continuous activity involving all levels of bank staff. Internal control is aimed at: (1) improving the effectiveness and efficiency of banking operations; (2) making financial information as reliable as possible; (3) preventing and detecting fraud and error; and (4) safeguarding the assets of banking institutions (BCBS, 1998). Internal control is supported by a number of different systems: accounting, internal audit, risk management, and credit review. They are all used for monitoring purposes in the internal control process.

A bank's internal control systems should be evaluated according to BCBS (1998), which states that an internal control system should be made up of five interrelated elements: (1) management oversight and control; (2) risk recognition and assessment; (3) control activities and segregation of duties; (4) information and communication; and (5) monitoring activities and correcting deficiencies.

Risk management is an important component in the management processes of a bank because of its close affinity to the continuity, stability, and prosperity of banks. The factors that influence the operational risk of banking institutions include globalization, increasing competition, new technologies and products, new markets and distribution channels, cultural diversity of staff and clients, and staff turnover. The stability of banking institutions depends on the extent to which managers are able to identify, measure, monitor and control different risks including liquidity risk, credit risk, concentration risk, interest rate risk, and exchange rate risk. Sound governance provides a good basis on which to ensure that risk management is effective. Thus, the procedures that need to be followed for internal control of risk management to be effective are explicitly identified in the governance guidelines.

The three elements involved in the management of risk in a banking institution are: (1) measuring and monitoring risk accurately; (2) controlling and putting a price on exposures; and (3) ensuring an adequate level of capital and reserves are held to deal with unexpected losses. The financial crisis of 2007 was the wake-up call banking regulatory and supervisory authorities needed to put in place appropriate policies to stop such crises occurring again. Bank managers have to face such risks as credit risk, interest rate risk, operational risk, and legal risk on a day-to-day basis. Guidelines as to how to manage these risks are given in BCBS (1998). The level of capitalization required to be held by banking institutions has been refined by the regulatory authorities in order to provide a cushion to absorb unexpected losses.

Conclusion

Corporate governance is an important topic for both non-financial firms and banking institutions. Understanding corporate governance issues is important to the management of firms and especially so for coordinating the relationship between different stakeholders and firm managers. This chapter begins by defining corporate governance from a number of perspectives and goes on to present theories that are relevant to corporate governance such as agency theory, stakeholder theory, and stewardship theory. The chapter then identifies the corporate governance problems of banks by discussing corporate governance structures, government safety nets, opaqueness, and market competition. This is followed by an overview of bank corporate governance in practice that focuses on two areas:ownership structure and governance, and internal governance mechanisms. As far as internal governance mechanisms are concerned, three topics are discussed: the board of directors, compensation of executives, and internal control.

Corporate governance is a topic that covers many fields of knowledge including economics, law, finance, management, sociology and politics, as reflected in the different views put forward at the beginning of the chapter. The three theories proposed – agency theory, stakeholder theory, and stewardship theory – agree with each other in terms of the complexity of company life. Each contributes to deeper understanding of corporate governance, despite having their own validity criteria and limitations. The agency problems in banking institutions are different from those in non-financial organizations. Corporate governance in banks is more complex than it is in non-financial institutions because it has to take the interests of the public into consideration. The duties and obligations of bank directors to ensure the security and soundness of banking institutions should be the focus of banking corporate governance. In other words, bank directors should be responsible not only to shareholders but to depositors, government, and the public as well. Government deposit protection guarantees together with the opacity of banking business have made moral hazard problems very serious in banking institutions, so much so that stricter regulation should be imposed on banks. Despite competition in banking being weaker than in non-financial firms, this is compensated for by internal mechanisms such as the regulation and supervision exercised by the board of directors as part of bank governance.

4

Risk management and performance in the Chinese banking sector

Abstract: As an important component of the financial system, the performance of the Chinese banking sector gets a lot of attention from the government, the banking regulatory authority, and bank managers. Empirical research in the banking sector uses different indicators to measure bank performance such as bank efficiency, bank productivity and bank profitability. Not only is the performance of Chinese commercial banks being paid a lot of attention, the Chinese government and the banking regulatory authorities are also concerned about the risk-taking behaviour of commercial banks. This chapter discusses the performance and risk condition of Chinese commercial banks, and the relationship between bank performance and bank risk is examined.

Key words: bank profitability, bank productivity, bank efficiency, bank risk, GMM, DEA, Tobit regression.

Introduction

Bank profitability, an indicator of bank performance, is a reflection of how banks are run given the environment in which they operate. Healthy and sustainable profitability plays a vital role in maintaining stability in the banking sector (Garcia-Herrero et al., 2009). However, it does not necessarily mean that profitability should be as high as possible because higher profitability may be an indicator of higher market power but lower competition, thus hindering improvements in efficiency and effective intermediation of savings. However, lower profitability not only discourages private agents from conducting banking activities, but decreases bank capacity to absorb negative shocks as well. According to annual reports from the China Banking Regulatory Commission (CBRC), the net profit after tax of the Chinese banking sector over the period 2003–11 constantly increased reaching a peak in 2011 of RMB0.13 trillion, a growth rate of 39.3 per cent over the previous year. The return on assets for the whole banking sector was 19.2 per cent, increasing by 1.7% compared with 2010, while the return on equity achieved at the end of 2011 was 1.2 per cent, a growth rate of 0.7 per cent over the previous year.

Bank efficiency, another indicator of bank performance, measures how inputs to the banking operation can be minimized to produce a certain amount of outputs or how to use a certain amount of inputs to maximize output production. This reflects management's skills at appropriately allocating input and output. Most empirical literature on the Chinese banking sector investigating efficiency finds that state-owned commercial banks (SOCBs) are the least efficient and relevant policies have been proposed on how to improve efficiency in the Chinese banking sector. An important performance indicator and an alternative measure to bank efficiency, bank productivity has received much attention from economists and policy makers and has been examined by empirical literature on European and transition economies (Athanasoglou et al., 2009; Delis et al., 2011). Similar to bank efficiency, bank productivity measures total output per unit input used in production. Banks that demonstrate higher productivity indicate they have the ability to produce a certain amount of outputs using fewer inputs or have the ability to use a given amount of inputs to produce a higher quantity of outputs.

Bank productivity places much greater emphasis on the impact technology has on bank production than does bank efficiency.

The financial crisis of 2007 represented a wake-up call for the government, the banking regulatory authority, and bank managers on the risk-taking behaviour of Chinese banks. As a result of China's unique banking industry, the operation of Chinese banks, especially SOCBs, is largely influenced by the central government, the consequence of which is a build-up of non-performing loans. The large volume of non-performing loans is a stumbling block to performance improvement of Chinese banks. The credit quality of Chinese banks has improved significantly during recent years. The non-performing loan ratio of all banking institutions was 1.77 per cent in 2011, 0.66 per cent lower than the previous year (CBRC, 2011). Although the figure in China was much lower than some banking sectors in European countries such as Ireland and Lithuania, where non-performing loan ratios were 16.1 and 16.3 per cent, respectively, it was still higher than Luxembourg, Finland, and Sweden, all of which had non-performing loan ratios below 1 per cent (EBF, 2012).

This chapter begins by looking at performance in the Chinese banking sector using efficiency/productivity and profitability as indicators. Second, the risks facing the Chinese banking sector are examined using different risk indicators such as the ratio between loan loss provisions and total loans, the Z-score, and stability inefficiency. Third, the determinants of bank profitability are tested with a focus on the impact of risk on bank profitability in China. Fourth, the technical efficiency/productivity of Chinese banks over the period 2003–11 is examined. Apart from shedding light on the efficiency of the three different types of ownerships of Chinese banks, the source of inefficiency and determinants of bank efficiency/productivity, especially the relationship between risk and efficiency/productivity, is evaluated.

This chapter is organized as follows: "Theory of bank performance" presents a theory on bank efficiency/ productivity and profitability. "Determinants of bank performance" explains the determinants of bank efficiency/ productivity and bank profitability. "Literature investigating bank performance in China" reviews the relevant literature on efficiency/productivity and profitability in the Chinese banking sector. "Methodology and data investigating the impact risk has on bank performance in China" describes the means used to measure the efficiency/productivity, risk indicators, and econometric estimation of the determinants of bank efficiency/productivity and profitability. There then follows a section entitled "Empirical results on the impact risk has on performance in the Chinese banking sector". The final section is entitled "Summary and conclusion".

Theory of bank performance

Theory of bank profitability

Just like other businesses, banks are profitable as long as their income exceeds their expenses. There are two main sources of bank income. The first source of bank income is classified as operating income which includes net gains on trading and derivatives, net gains on other securities, net insurance income as well as net fees and commissions, while the second source of bank income is interest income which indicates the interest it earns on its assets. The main sources of expenses are the interest it pays on its liabilities and non-interest expenses such as personnel and operating expenses. The major assets of a bank include loans to individuals, businesses, and other organizations and the securities it holds. The major liabilities of a bank are its deposits and money that it borrows, either from customers, other banks and other short-term borrowings.

The recent empirical literature on banking uses a number of different measures as profitability indicators: return on assets (ROA), return on equity (ROE), net interest margin (NIM), and profit margin (PBT).

ROA is defined as the ratio between net income and total assets. It reflects a bank's ability to utilize assets to gain net profit. A low ratio indicates that a bank is relatively less efficient at converting the money it invested into net income. ROE, on the other hand, reflects a bank's ability to generate income using shareholder funds. It is calculated by dividing a bank's net income by shareholder equity. The higher the ratio the more efficient a bank's utilization of shareholder funds. Although ROE is commonly used in the financial literature, it is not the best profitability indicator for the following reasons. First, banks with a higher level of equity (lower leverage) normally have a higher ROA but a lower ROE. Second, ROE disregards the higher risk that is associated with higher leverage and the effect of regulation on leverage (Dietrich and Wanzenried, 2011). NIM reflects how successful a bank's investment decisions are relative to its interest expenses. It is expressed by using the difference between interest income generated and the amount of interest paid out divided by interest-earning assets. A negative value indicates that a bank's investment decisions are not optimal because interest expenses are more than interest income generated through loans.

In addition to these widely used profitability indicators, some researchers use other profitability indicators. Profit margin is used in a few empirical studies to measure bank profitability (Demirguc-Kunt and Huizinga, 1999b; Bashir, 2003; Aburime, 2009; Amba and Almukharreq, 2013). It is defined as the ratio between a bank's earnings before tax and total assets. It is an indicator of how efficiently a bank uses its assets to generate earnings before contractual obligations must be paid. The higher the ratio the more efficient the bank at utilising assets to generate earnings.

Theory of bank efficiency

A simple measure of firm efficiency is defined by Farrell (1957) whose work was based on Debreu (1951) and Koopmans (1951). He argued that technical efficiency reflects a firm's ability to obtain maximal output from a given set of inputs. Farrell explained his idea by making the assumption that firms use two inputs (X_1 and X_2) to produce one output (y), and that production is under the assumption of constant return to scale (CRS) (see Figure 4.1). In other words, an increase (decrease) in the inputs leads to the same proportional increase (decrease) in the output. The unit isoquant SS' describes the technological set necessary to produce a certain amount of output using a combination of inputs (X_1 and X_2). In other words, SS' shows the minimum amount of inputs needed to produce one unit of output. All production along this curve SS' is supposed to be perfectly efficient, while any other points above or located to the

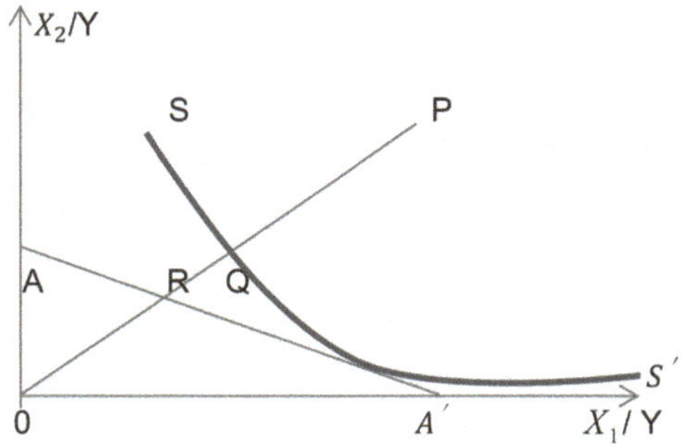

Figure 4.1 **The measurement of technical efficiency**

Source: Coelli (1996).

right of the curve, such as point *P*, are regarded as inefficient production because the amount of inputs used to produce one unit of output is more than those needed for efficient production.

Distance *QP* represents the technical inefficiency of the firm. It also represents the amount of inputs that can be reduced without any influence on output production. In other words, it represents the amount of inputs that can be reduced without any decrease in output. The input reduction/technical inefficiency percentage level for point *P* can be represented by the ratio $QP/0P$, while the technical efficiency of a firm can be measured by the ratio $0Q/0P$. The value of technical efficiency ranges from 0 and 1. A value of 1 means that the firm is fully technically efficient.

The condition necessary for CRS to be assumed is that all firms are operating optimally, which is, of course, very often impossible because of imperfect competition. Variable return to scale (VRS) further decomposes technical efficiency into pure technical efficiency (PTE) and scale efficiency (SE). In Figure 4.2 it is assumed that firms use one input *X* to produce one output *Y*. In the figure the CRS frontier is represented by *CRS*, the

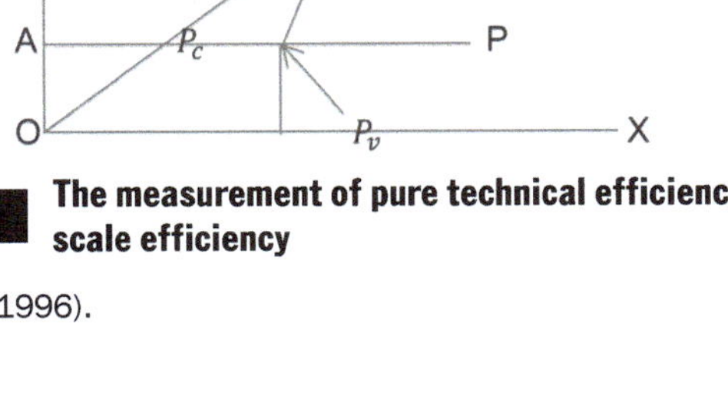

Figure 4.2 **The measurement of pure technical efficiency and scale efficiency**

Source: Coelli (1996).

production of a firm lies either on the curve or locates to the right of it, the technical inefficiency of firm P is PP_c/AP, and technical efficiency is represented by the ratio AP_c/AP.

Scale efficiency considers the possibility that firms do not operate at the optimal size. By replacing the CRS assumption by the VRS assumption, scale efficiency can be measured. The VRS frontier is represented by *VRS*, under which the technical inefficiency of firm *P* is PP_v/AP, its pure technical efficiency is represented by the ratio AP_v/AP, and scale efficiency is represented by the ratio AP_c/AP_v. If the firm operates under CRS, the value of scale efficiency equals one, while the value of scale efficiency will be less than one in a VRS situation. In other words, firms have scale inefficiency.

Theory of bank productivity

The concept of total factor productivity was first developed by Tinbergen (1942) and Stigler (1947) and a reference framework for the main empirical approaches to total factor productivity was created by Solow (1957). This framework argues that total factor productivity is a residual attributable to innovation and technological and organizational improvement that cannot be explained by changes in inputs.

There are three principal views of total factor productivity in the empirical literature. The first, held by a number of authors including Barro (1999), is that total factor productivity reflects a shift in the production function arising from technological progress. Griliches (1987) further argues that production technology can be defined as a means of converting inputs into outputs. Changes in the production technology of banking include changes to many aspects of banking such as type and quality of outputs, progress in scientific production and managerial techniques. The second view's main proponent is Balk (2001) who suggests that total factor productivity mainly reflects an improvement in efficiency of the production unit. He argues that the total factor productivity of a firm or an industry may be increased by simply allocating inputs more appropriately and efficiently, resulting in production getting very close to the optimum combination of inputs and outputs; in other words, total factor productivity can be increased without improving technology. The last of our three views is held by Jorgenson and Griliches (1967) who argue that total factor productivity focusses on the effect economies of scale have on changing the scale of operation of a firm or industry. In the banking industry there are different inputs such as capital, labour, and funds and there are also different outputs such as interest income derived from traditional loan–deposit services and non-interest income earned from non-traditional activities. Total factor productivity reflects changes in the composition of the output and input mix.

Determinants of bank performance

Determinants influencing bank profitability

This section investigates sources of bank profitability. In other words, it reviews the relevant literature regarding investigation of the determinants of profitability in the banking sector. To be more specific, the determinants of bank profitability are broken down into three groups: bank-specific determinants, industry-specific determinants, and the macroeconomic environment.

Bank-specific determinants

According to empirical research, bank profitability is affected by a number of bank-specific determinants such as bank size, liquidity, capitalization, risk, cost management, non-traditional activity, and labour productivity.

- *Bank size*: bank size can be measured by the natural logarithm of total assets. The empirical literature puts forward different arguments on the impact bank size has on bank profitability. On the one hand, costs can be reduced for larger banks because of economies of scale and scope. This opinion is supported by a number of scholars such as Bourke, 1989; Molyneux and Thornton, 1992; Akhavein et al., 1997; Bikker and Hu, 2002; and Goddard et al., 2004. However, large banks are made up of comprehensive branches and representative offices in different cities and different countries around the world, which makes it harder to manage them, the resultant increase in costs leads to a decline in bank profitability. The effect of bank size on bank profitability is non-linear as suggested by Eichengreen and Gibson (2001) who argue that bank profitability will increase as size increases, but only to a certain point. Beyond this point profitability will decrease. So there is no *a priori* expectation regarding the effect of bank size on bank profitability.

- *Liquidity*: liquidity measures the extent to which a bank can fulfil its obligations when they become due. The ratio between total loans and total assets can be used to measure this variable. The higher the ratio the larger the proportion of assets used to make loans, which suggests the bank has lower liquidity. Bourke (1989) argues that liquidity can have a negative impact on bank profitability because the lower the liquidity the higher the volume of loans, which increases interest income and further improves bank profitability. However, Graham and Bordelean (2010) suggest that the impact of bank liquidity on bank profitability is non-linear; in other words, any increase in the liquidity level increases bank profitability, while bank profitability starts decreasing if bank liquidity is above a certain point. So there is no *a priori* expectation regarding the influence of liquidity on bank profitability.

- *Capitalization*: capitalization indicates the proportion of assets attributed to money contributed by shareholders. It can be measured using the ratio between shareholder equity and total assets. It is considered an important determinant of bank profitability. Berger (1995a) argues that capitalization can have a negative impact on bank profitability because the higher the level of capitalization the lower the relative risk position of the bank. According to the risk–return trade-off, lower risk leads to lower return. However, there are researchers who believe that capitalization has a positive impact on bank profitability. For example, Molyneux (1993) argues that funding costs can be lower for banks with higher levels of capitalization because the larger the share of capital the higher the creditworthiness of the bank. Berger (1995b) argues that expected earnings can be raised and the expected cost of financial distress can be reduced by increasing the level of capitalization. Furthermore, as a cushion to absorb risk, higher levels of capital enable banks to make additional loans and, hence, increase bank profitability. So there is no *a priori* expectation regarding the effect of capitalization on bank profitability.

- *Bank risk*: bank risk can be measured by the ratio between loan loss provisions and total loans. This measurement is complemented by two alternative indicators: the Z-score and stability inefficiency.[1] The higher the ratio between loan loss provisions and total loans the higher the bank risk; the higher the Z-score the lower the bank risk; and the higher the stability inefficiency the higher the bank risk. As discussed earlier, higher risk is normally accompanied by higher returns, which is in line with the traditional risk–return hypothesis. However, this hypothesis is only applicable when a bank has a complete risk check, monitoring, and management system. Lack of ability to manage risk effectively will incur greater costs and reduce bank profitability. After several rounds of banking reforms in China, Chinese banks are now believed to have more experience in risk management. In other words, now that the traditional risk–return hypothesis is applicable to the Chinese banking sector, so it is expected that those Chinese commercial banks running higher risks will normally be more profitable.

- *Cost management*: cost management can be measured by the ratio between overhead and total assets. Jiang et al. (2003) argues that operating expenses can have a negative impact on bank profitability because efficiency can be improved by reducing expenses and cost reduction derived from higher efficiency can improve bank profitability. However, the positive relationship between expenses and bank profitability is supported by Molyneux and Thornton (1992), Guru et al. (2002), and Ben Naceur (2003). They argue that a large proportion of expenses is attributed to the salary and wages paid to staff. Banks pay higher salaries and wages to experienced staff to get them to work harder and thereby increase the productivity needed for an improvement in bank profitability. This opinion is in line with the efficiency wage theory. Furthermore, they argue that banks can pass expenses on to borrowers and depositors by raising the loan interest rate and decreasing the deposit interest rate. So there is no *a priori* expectation regarding cost management and bank profitability.

- *Non-traditional activity*: non-traditional activity can be measured by the ratio between non-interest income and gross revenue. More income resources can be generated by activity diversification. The greater the number of services provided by a bank the lower its reliance on interest income generated from traditional loan–deposit services that can be negatively affected by an economic downturn. Therefore, this variable is expected to have a positive impact on bank profitability. However, Demirguc-Kunt and Huizinga (1999) suggest there is a negative relationship between the volume of non-traditional activity and bank profitability. They explain their opinion by pointing to the existence of higher competition in non-traditional service areas such as insurance writing and investment banking; higher competition dampens bank profitability. So there is no *a priori* expectation regarding the effect of non-traditional activity on bank profitability.

- *Labour productivity*: labour productivity can be measured by the ratio between gross revenue and number of employees. Athanasoglou et al. (2008) argue that labour productivity has a positive impact on bank profitability in Greece. The higher the level of labour productivity the higher the volume of revenue generated per employee, which is supposed to increase bank profitability. So, the impact labour productivity has on bank profitability is expected to be significant and positive.

Industry-specific determinants

Bank profitability is not only affected by bank-specific determinants, developments in relevant industries can also influence bank profitability. The empirical literature focusses on three determinants: banking sector concentration, banking sector development, and stock market development.

- *Banking sector concentration*: banking sector concentration is a measurement of the relative size of assets held by a few of the largest banks in relation to the assets of the whole banking sector. Normally, a three-bank or five-bank concentration ratio is considered a good proxy. It is measured by the ratio between the largest three/five banks' assets and the assets of the whole banking industry. Banking sector concentration has a positive impact on bank profitability, as argued by Smirlock (1985) and Staikouras and Wood (2003). A highly concentrated banking market increases the monopolistic power of a bank, which leads to an improvement in bank profitability. This is in line with the Structure–Conduct–Performance (SCP) hypothesis that suggests banks in a higher concentrated market tend to collude with each other to obtain supernormal profits. However, there are a few researchers whose findings are at odds with the SCP hypothesis. For instance, Ben Naceur (2003) argues that in a higher concentrated banking market, bank profitability in Tunisia was lower. So there is no *a priori* expectation regarding the influence of banking sector concentration on bank profitability.

- *Banking sector development*: banking sector development plays an important role in bank profitability. It can be measured by the ratio between banking sector assets and GDP. Many researchers have investigated whether financial structure plays a role in determining bank performance. In general, the higher the banking-assets-to-GDP ratio the more important the role played by financial development in the economy. This relative importance may reflect a higher demand for banking services, which in turn may attract potential competitors to enter the market. Higher competition is supposed to decrease bank profitability. Demirguc-Kunt and Huizinga (1999) argue that banks in countries that have more competitive banking sectors, where bank assets contribute to GDP in a major way, generally have smaller margins and less profitability. So the expectation is that this variable has a negative impact on bank profitability.

- *Stock market development*: stock market development is another part of the financial system that can influence bank profitability. Demirguc-Kunt and Huizinga (1999) argue that bank profitability is higher in countries where there is a well-developed stock market. They give a couple of reasons to explain the positive impact stock market development has on bank profitability: (1) a well-developed stock market provides more opportunities for firms to obtain funds from equity finance, which decreases the number of non-performing loans, increases borrowing capacity, and better capitalizes banks; (2) a well-developed stock market provides more information about publicly traded firms, which is very useful for banks to evaluate and monitor risk. Better evaluation of bank risk reduces the number of non-performing loans and makes higher profitability possible. So the expectation is that stock market development has a significant and positive impact on bank profitability.

Macroeconomic determinants

- *Inflation*: the annual inflation rate is an important determinant of bank profitability. Its impact on bank profitability depends on whether inflation is anticipated or not (Perry, 1992). The relationship between bank profitability and inflation is positive as long as inflation is fully anticipated and the interest rate is adjusted accordingly. Therefore, revenues increase faster than costs, which leads to an improvement in bank profitability. Pasiouras and Kosmidou (2007), Athanasoglou et al. (2008), and Garcia-Herrero et al. (2009) report the positive impact inflation has had on bank profitability in the EU, Greece, and China, respectively. So the expectation is that inflation has a positive impact on bank profitability.

- *GDP growth rate*: economic growth is believed to influence bank profitability. The annual GDP growth rate is the indicator. During recessions the demand for lending decreases and the probability of default increases, which leads to a drop in bank profitability (Athanasoglou et al., 2008.; Dietrich and Wanzenried, 2011). However, Liu et al. (2013) argue that higher economic growth both improves the business environment and lowers bank entry barriers. The consequent increase in competition dampens bank profitability. So there is no *a priori* expectation regarding the influence of GDP growth rate on bank profitability.

Determinants that affect bank efficiency/productivity

Like the determinants of bank profitability, the determinants of bank efficiency/productivity can also be divided into three groups: bank-specific determinants, industry-specific determinants, and macroeconomic determinants. Bank-specific determinants mainly include bank size, bank risk, bank liquidity, non-traditional activity, bank capitalization, labour productivity, and overhead cost. Industry-specific determinants include bank competition (banking sector concentration), banking sector development, and stock market development. The two macroeconomic variables believed to influence bank efficiency/productivity are inflation and GDP growth.

Bank size is expected to have a positive impact on bank efficiency/productivity; this variable is included to capture possible cost advantages associated with size (larger banks in terms of total assets can decrease costs as a result of economies of scale, which increases efficiency/productivity). The bad luck hypothesis states that any increase in risk leads to additional costs and managerial effort; so the expectation is that risk has a negative impact on bank efficiency/productivity. Liquidity is an indication of a bank's ability to meet the daily cash needs of its customers and respond to sudden withdrawals. The higher the ability (lower figures) the lower the bankruptcy cost. So the expectation is that this variable is negatively related to bank efficiency/productivity. There is no *a priori* expectation regarding the influence of non-traditional activity on bank efficiency/productivity in China. On the one hand, banks engaging in a range of business activities can benefit from and decrease operational costs by economies of scope. However, on the other hand and as discussed earlier, there is higher competition in the non-traditional business area, the resultant increase in competition leads to higher risk-taking by Chinese banks, and the increase in the cost of monitoring risk leads to a decline in bank efficiency/productivity. Thus, there is no *a priori* expectation of this variable. Capitalization is expected to have a positive impact on bank efficiency/productivity. As argued by Jeitschko and Jeung (2005), better capitalized banks have fewer moral hazard incentives and are more likely to adopt careful practices to reduce cost. Labour productivity measures the number of bank outputs per unit of labour; the higher the value of this variable the higher the output-to-input ratio. So, this variable is expected to affect bank efficiency/productivity positively. Overhead cost measures a bank's ability to control various costs. Banks with lower overhead costs are clearly more able to control many aspects of cost, which leads to higher efficiency/ productivity (Girardone et al., 2004). So the expectation is that the impact of overhead cost on bank efficiency/productivity is significant and negative.

In the Chinese banking sector any increase in competition (lower banking sector concentration) induces bank managers to be more careful when controlling inputs, the resulting reduction in cost improves efficiency/productivity; thus, banking sector concentration is expected to be negatively correlated with bank efficiency/productivity. Banking sector development is believed to have a negative impact on bank efficiency/productivity. As discussed earlier, the demand for banking services is greater when there is a better developed banking sector, which attracts potential competitors to enter the market; the stronger the competition the greater the incentive for bank managers to improve efficiency/productivity. There is no *a priori* expectation of stock market development on bank efficiency/productivity. As the stock market expands, more businesses/companies will raise funds from the stock market rather than banks, thus decreasing bank output. So efficiency/ productivity will be negatively affected. However, on the other hand and as discussed earlier, the availability of information about publicly listed firms will be improved when there is a better developed stock market, the resulting improved transparency regarding the credit condition of firms reduces the default rate and monitoring costs of banks, which leads to better bank efficiency/productivity. Inflation is expected to affect bank efficiency/productivity negatively because under inflationary conditions banks might feel less pressure to control inputs and therefore become less efficient (Akmal and Saleem, 2008). The impact of GDP growth on bank efficiency/ productivity is believed to be significant and positive. As discussed in the "Theory of bank profitability" subsection, the higher the growth in GDP the greater the reduction in the loan default rate, which further decreases bank costs and improves bank efficiency/productivity. Furthermore, the higher the growth in GDP the greater the chance of potential competitors entering the market. More competition is supposed to have a favourable effect on bank efficiency/productivity.

Literature investigating bank performance in China

Research into bank profitability in China

There are a number of researchers who have investigated bank profitability in China and its determinants. Heffernan and Fu (2010) evaluate the determinants of bank profitability in China from 1999 to 2006; the results indicate that bank listings and efficiency have helped increase bank profitability in China. As far as bank-specific determinants are concerned, they suggest that size and non-traditional activity have no impact on bank profitability in China, whereas as far as the macroeconomic environment is concerned, the research indicates that bank profitability in China is significantly affected by the real GDP growth rate. The determinants of profitability of four state-owned and twelve joint stock commercial banks (JSCBs) from 2000 to 2007 are examined by Sufian (2009a). The findings suggest that Chinese banks that are bigger in terms of total assets, higher risk levels, and capital levels normally have higher profitability, whereas the profitability of Chinese banks is significantly and negatively affected by bank liquidity level and overhead cost. They finally report that economic booms and higher inflation result in increased bank profitability. The determinants of profitability of a sample of

Chinese banks between 2000 to 2005 are also evaluated by Sufian and Habibullah (2009). The results indicate that profitability is significantly and positively affected by bank liquidity, risk level, and capital level. They further suggest that bigger city commercial banks (CCBs) where control over costs leaves much to be desired have lower profitability, while city commercial banks that have higher capital levels and engage in more diversified business activities (higher volumes of non-traditional activity) normally have higher profitability.

The low profitability of Chinese banks between 1997 and 2004 is explained by Garcia-Herrero et al. (2009). The results indicate that Chinese banks with higher levels of capital, a higher level of efficiency, and larger shares of overall deposits normally have higher profitability, whereas the profitability of Chinese banks is relatively low in a more concentrated banking market. Their findings further suggest that JSCBs outperform SOCBs, the main drag on Chinese bank profitability. The effect of ownership on bank profitability in China between 1997 and 2004 is analysed in Lin and Zhang (2009) using a range of Chinese banks; the results indicate that the Big 4 state-owned banks[2] are less profitable and have poorer asset quality than other types of banks.

More recent research into the determinants of bank profitability in China have been undertaken by Tan and Floros (2012a, b). The effect of inflation on bank profitability from 2003 to 2009 is examined by Tan and Floros (2012a), while controlling for comprehensive bank-specific and industry-specific determinants. They argue that bank profitability is significantly and negatively affected by the volume of non-traditional activity and overhead cost. They find that Chinese bank profitability is relatively higher in banking and stock markets that are better developed. Higher inflation rates also improve bank profitability. Tan and Floros (2012b) focus on the impact GDP growth rate has on bank profitability. They argue that Chinese bank profitability is relatively lower at times of economic boom.

Research into bank efficiency/productivity in China

There are few pieces of research investigating the efficiency/ productivity of the Chinese banking industry over the period 1997 to 2006. Sufian and Majid (2009) look particularly at the relationship between technical efficiency and share price performance. The authors control for several bank-specific factors that are believed to impact technical efficiency over the period 1997 to 2006. The results indicate that larger Chinese banks in terms of total assets normally have higher technical and pure technical efficiency, whereas the scale efficiency of medium-sized banks is relatively higher. The study suggests that there is a positive relationship between share price performance and efficiency scores. The impact of non-traditional activities on the technical, pure technical, and scale efficiency of state-owned and joint-stock commercial banks in China over the period 2000 to 2005 is examined by Sufian (2009b). The empirical results suggest that the improvement in scale efficiency contributed to the enhancement of the technical efficiency of Chinese SOCBs when non-traditional activity attributed to improvements in scale efficiency is included, whereas improvements in pure technical efficiency contributed more to the higher technical efficiency of JSCBs.

The effect of banking reforms on technical efficiency and change in total factor productivity in the Chinese banking industry between 1993 and 2002 is analysed by Kumbhakar and Wang (2007). The results indicate that JSCBs are more efficient than SOCBs, and that productivity growth in JSCBs was higher than in SOCBs over the examined period. Technical efficiency is also examined by Jiang et al. (2009) over the period 1995 to 2005. The results indicate that the efficiency of domestic banks can be improved by foreign acquisition, while initial public offerings have only a short-term effect on improvements in efficiency in Chinese banks.

Cao (2007) investigates the technical efficiency of 4 Chinese SOCBs and 10 JSCBs between 2001 and 2003. The results suggest that the technical efficiency of Chinese commercial banks has improved and that JSCBs are more efficient than SOCBs. Laurenceson and Zhao (2008) examine the efficiency level of 11 Chinese banks over the period 2003–07. The findings show the difference in the efficiency level among the banks examined is quite small, although a number of major banks have lower efficiency; they also show the efficiency of most of the less prominent banks lags that of their counterparts. The efficiency of 11 nationwide banks over the period 1995–2004 is investigated by Hu et al. (2009). The findings suggest that the efficiency of Chinese SOCBs can be improved by bringing about ownership reform. The technical efficiency of 43 Chinese commercial banks from 1993 to 2000 is examined by Chen et al. (2005). The results show that the efficiency of medium-sized Chinese banks is lower than that of large and small banks.

Methodology and data investigating the impact risk has on bank performance in China

Methodology used to estimate bank risk in China

In this section the procedure used to estimate two risk indicators – the Z-score and stability inefficiency – are presented. There then follows an explanation of econometric estimation which can be used to ascertain the determinants of bank profitability.

Methodology used to measure the Z-score in the Chinese banking sector

The Z-score was proposed by Hanna and Hanweck (1988) to measure the level of exposure of financial institutions to insolvency risk. It is now widely used in the banking sector (Hesse and Cihak, 2007; Iannotta et al., 2007; Beck et al., 2009; Liu and Wilson 2013). This indicator considers that the risk of failure depends fundamentally on the interaction between income-generating capacity, the potential magnitude of return shocks, and the level of capital reserves (Garcia-Marco and Robles-Fernandez, 2008). The Z-score can be calculated as:

$$Z = \frac{ROA + E/A}{\sigma(ROA)} \tag{4.1}$$

where ROA is the bank's return on assets; E/A is the equity-to-total assets ratio; and $\sigma(ROA)$ is the standard deviation of the return on assets. Banks with higher profitability and capital levels relative to the volatility of return normally have higher figures for this indicator and, thus, lower risk and greater stability.

Methodology to measure stability efficiency in the Chinese banking sector

Fang et al. (2011) argue that the potential stability of banks is not necessarily reflected by the Z-score. Any deviation of a bank's current stability from the maximum stability stipulated by economic and regulatory conditions must be considered. In this section the stability inefficiency of a bank is given by estimating a stochastic frontier (Aigner et al., 1977; Meeusen and Van den Broeck, 1977) with the Z-score as the dependent variable of the translog[3] specification. The equation used to stimate the frontier is as follows:

$$Ln\left(\frac{Z\text{-}score}{W_2}\right)_{it} = \delta_0 + \sum_j \delta_j \, Ln\, Y_{jit} + \frac{1}{2}\sum_j \sum_k \delta_{jk} \, Ln\, Y_{jit} \, Ln\, Y_{kit}$$
$$+ \beta_1 \, Ln\left(\frac{W_1}{W_2}\right)_{it} + \frac{1}{2}\beta_2 \, Ln\left(\frac{W_1}{W_2}\right)_{it}$$
$$+ \sum_j \theta_j \, Ln\, Y_{jit} \, Ln\left(\frac{W_1}{W_2}\right)_{it} + v_{it} - u_{it} \qquad (4.2)$$

where W is the input price – the two input prices considered are the price of funds (interest expenses to total deposits) and the price of capital (non-interest expenses to total assets); Y represents four outputs (total loans, total deposits, other earning assets, and non-interest income); sub-indices i and t represent bank i operating at time t, while j and k represent different outputs; and the error term ε_{it} equals $v_{it} - u_{it}$. The first term v_{it} captures random disturbance which is assumed to be normally distributed and represents measurement errors and other uncontrolled factors (i.e., $v_{it} \sim N(0, \sigma_v^2)$). The second term u_{it} captures technical and allocative inefficiency, both under managerial control, and is assumed to be half-normally distributed (i.e., $u_{it} \sim N^+(\mu_{it}, \sigma_v^2)$). The higher the stability inefficiency the greater the bank risk, while the lower the stability inefficiency the more stable the bank.

Estimating the determinants of bank profitability: the Generalized Method of Moments

There are a number of methods used by the empirical literature to examine the determinants of bank profitability. The fixed effect estimator is used by Maudos and Fernandez de Guevara (2004) and Kosmidou et al. (2006) to investigate the determinants of bank profitability in the EU and the UK, respectively, while the Generalized Least Squares (GLS) method is used by Hassan and Bashir (2003) to assess the determinants of Islamic bank profitability between 1994 and 2001. However, most researchers today use the Generalized Method of Moments (GMM) estimator to examine the determinants of bank profitability (Athanasoglou et al., 2008; Garcia-Herrero et al., 2009; Goddard et al., 2011; Dietrich and Wanzenried, 2011). They argue that there are a number of problems that make the fixed effect estimator and GLS unsuitable for the estimation.

The first problem is endogeneity. Equity may be able to be increased by more profitable banks through retaining profits. On the other hand, they may choose to spend more money on advertising campaigns that will impact bank profitability. However, causality could take the opposite route with more personnel being hired by banks with higher profitability, which in return reduces operational efficiency.

The second problem is unobservable heterogeneity across banks which may be extensive among Chinese banks given differences in corporate governance. Finally, the degree of profitability could be very persistent as a result of government interference. In the Chinese banking industry, the central government still has strong influence on the operation of commercial banks, especially SOCBs, not only in terms of credit allocation but also the protection provided by the government to SOCBs through a variety of forms to make them achieve higher profits such as capital injection, and writing off non-performing loans. So the expectation is that Chinese bank profitability is persistent to some extent.

In an effort to solve these problems, Arellano and Bond (1991) developed the difference GMM estimator, which uses all available lagged values of dependent variables and lagged values of exogenous regressors as instruments. This method is criticized by Arellano and Bover (1995) and Blundell and Bond (1998) who argue that the GMM difference estimator is inefficient if the instruments are weak. Hence, they developed a new method, the system GMM estimator, which includes lagged levels as well as lagged differences. Roodman (2006) argues that the difference GMM and system GMM estimators can solve the problems of endogeneity, unobserved heterogeneity, and profit persistence. Bond (2002) argues that the unit root[4] property biases the difference GMM estimator while the system GMM estimator yields results with greater precision.

The following GMM proposed by Athanasoglou et al. (2008) is used for empirical analysis of this study, which empirically examines the extent to which the profitability of Chinese banks is influenced by internal factors (bank-specific determinants) and external factors (industry and macroeconomic determinants):

$$\Pi_{it} = C + \delta II_{i,\tau-1} + \sum_{j=1}^{j} \beta_j X^j_{it} + \sum_{l=1}^{l} \beta_l X^l_{it} + \sum_{m-1}^{m} \beta_m X^m_{it} + \varepsilon_{it} \qquad (4.3)$$

$$\varepsilon_{it} = \mu_{it} + \nu_{it} \qquad (4.4)$$

where Π_{it} is the profitability of bank i at year t measured by ROA, ROE, NIM and PBT; $II_{i,t-1}$ is one-period lagged profitability, which is included to test whether profitability in the Chinese banking sector persists over time; δ is the speed of adjustment, which ranges from 0 to 1 – a δ value close to 0 indicates that the industry is relatively competitive (high speed of adjustment), while a δ close to 1 suggests that industry is relatively less competitive (low speed of adjustment); X^j_{it} are the bank-specific determinants of profitability which include size, liquidity, capitalization, risk, overhead cost, non-traditional activity, and labour productivity; X^l_{it} are the industry-specific determinants of profitability, which include banking sector concentration, banking sector development, and stock market development; X^m_{it} are the macroeconomic determinants of bank profitability, which include the annual inflation rate and annual GDP growth rate; μ_{it} is an unobserved bank-specific time-invariant effect; and ν_{it} is a disturbance term that is independent across banks.

Methodology used to estimate the impact of risk on bank efficiency/productivity in China

Our focus in this subsection is to explain the methods used to test the impact risk has on bank efficiency/productivity in China. We begin by looking at the methodology used to measure the technical efficiency of Chinese banks. Then we embark on a discussion of the methodology used to measure the productivity of Chinese banks. Finally, we consider the econometric method used to estimate the impact risk has on bank efficiency/productivity.

Methodology used to estimate technical efficiency in Chinese banking sector

There are two principal methods to measure bank efficiency: parametric and non-parametric. A typical parametric estimation is the stochastic frontier approach (SFA), whereas a typical non-parametric method is data envelopment analysis (DEA), which is widely used to investigate bank efficiency.

The SFA was developed by Aigner et al. (1977), and was applied to banks by Ferrier and Lovell (1990). It specifies a particular form of cost function, usually a translog, and allows for random errors. The SFA assumes that these errors consist of inefficiencies that follow an asymmetric distribution, usually a truncated or half-normal distribution, and random errors that follow a symmetric distribution, usually the standard normal distribution. It is criticized for its pre-specified functional form and distributional assumption (Fries and Taci, 2005). Furthermore, it is likely that regulations and other market imperfections distort prices in the Chinese banking sector complicating the application of SFA to price and quantity data, which makes SFA unsuitable as a tool to estimate technical efficiency in the Chinese banking sector.

The efficiency estimates in this study were obtained using data envelopment analysis (DEA). DEA, also known as the CCR model after its proponents (Charnes, Cooper, and Rhodes, 1978), is a linear programming technique. The CCR model measures the efficiency of each decision-making unit (DMU) obtained as a maximum of the ratio between weighted outputs and weighted inputs. In other words, the fewer the inputs invested in producing the given output, the more efficient the production. DEA has a number of advantages: (1) it is able to handle multiple inputs and outputs given in different measurement units; (2) it does not require any assumptions about the distribution of inefficiency (Charnes et al., 1995); (3) it works particularly well with small samples (Maudos et al., 2002). The CCR model presupposes that there is no significant relationship between the scale of operation and efficiency by assuming a constant return to scale (CRS). The CRS assumption is only suitable when all DMUs are operating optimally.

Banker et al. (1984) extend the CCR model by relaxing the CRS assumption. The resulting BCC model – named after its proponents, Banker, Charnes, and Cooper – is used to assess the efficiency of DMUs characterized by a variable return to scale (VRS). The VRS assumption allows measurement of pure technical efficiency (PTE) (i.e., the measurement of technical efficiency devoid of the scale efficiency effect). The CCR model can be expressed as:

$$\left.\begin{array}{c}\min_{\theta,\lambda} \theta, \\ \text{subject to} \\ -y_i + Y\lambda \geq 0, \theta x_i - X\lambda \geq 0, \lambda \geq 0\end{array}\right\} \quad (4.5)$$

where θ is a scalar; λ is a $n \times 1$ vector of constants; Y represents all input and output data for N firms; x_i are individual inputs; and y_i are outputs for the ith firm. The efficiency score for each DMU is given by θ; it takes a value between 0 and 1, which indicates the efficiency level.

The CRS linear programming problem can easily be modified to account for VRS by adding the convexity constraint, $N1'\lambda = 1$:

$$\left.\begin{array}{c}\min_{\theta,\lambda} \theta, \\ \text{subject to} \\ -y_i + Y\lambda \geq 0, \theta x_i - X\lambda \geq 0, N1'\lambda = 1, \lambda \geq 0\end{array}\right\} \quad (4.6)$$

where $N1$ is an $N \times 1$ vector of ones. This approach forms a convex hull of intersecting planes that envelop the data points more tightly than a CRS conical hull; this provides pure technical efficiency scores that are greater than or equal to those obtained using the CRS model. If the efficiency scores obtained from the CRS model and VRS model are different, this indicates that the DMU has scale inefficiency and that scale inefficiency can be calculated from the difference between the VRS technical efficiency score and the CRS technical efficiency score. The relationship between CRS and VRS is given as:

$$TE_{CRS} = TE_{VRS} \times SE \quad (4.7)$$

Methodology used to estimate productivity in the Chinese banking sector

The output-oriented Malmquist method defined by Caves et al. (1982) is used to derive total factor productivity (TFP) growth. Fare et al. (2004) use DEA to estimate total factor productivity. This is the most popular non-parametric approach used to obtain TFP growth estimates. Let us introduce some notation. Assume there are n observations using m inputs to produce L outputs. Each observation n uses a non-negative vector of inputs denoted $X^n = (X_1^n, X_2^n, \ldots, X_m^n) \in R^m$ to produce a non-negative vector of outputs denoted $Y^n = (Y_1^n, Y_2^n, \ldots, Y_l^n) \in R^L$. The production technology can be written as:

$$F = \{(Y, X) : X \; canproduce \; Y\}$$

which describes a set of feasible input–output vectors. The input sets of production technology can be written as:

$$PT(Y) = \{X : (Y, X) \in F\}$$

which describes the sets of input vectors that are feasible for each output vector. The output Malmquist TFP index can then be expressed as:

$$M_0(x^s, y^s, x^t, y^t) = \left[\frac{D_0^s(x^t, y^t)}{D_0^s(x^s, y^s)} \frac{D_0^t(x^t, y^t)}{D_0^t(x^s, y^s)}\right]^{1/2} \tag{4.8}$$

where M_0 measures the productivity change between periods s and t; $D_0^s(x^t, y^t)$ represents the distance from period t observation to period s technology; $M_0 > 1$ indicates positive TFP growth from period s to period t; $M_0 < 1$ indicates a decline; and $M_0 = 1$ indicates constant TFP growth.

Examination of the impact risk has on the technical efficiency of Chinese banks

In order to test the relationship between risk and technical efficiency/productivity in the Chinese banking sector, the two-step approach of Coelli et al. (1998) is followed. Using the technical efficiency/productivity derived from DEA as the dependent variable, the following Tobit regression model can be estimated:

$$\begin{aligned}\theta_{it} = C + \beta_1 \, bankspecific_{it} + \beta_2 \, industryspecific_{it} \\ + \beta_3 \, macroeconomic + \varepsilon_{it}\end{aligned} \tag{4.9}$$

where C is the constant term; i, t represent a specific bank in a specific year; *bankspecific* are bank-specific variables affecting technical efficiency such as bank size, liquidity, capitalization, risk, overhead cost, non-traditional activity, and labour productivity; *industryspecific* are industry-specific variables influencing technical efficiency/productivity such as banking sector concentration, banking sector development, and stock market development; *macroeconomic* are two macroeconomic determinants of bank efficiency: annual inflation rate and annual GDP growth rate; and ε_{it} is the error term.

The two principal methods used in the banking literature to investigate the determinants of efficiency are the ordinary least squares (OLS) method (Sufian and Habibullah, 2010) and Tobit regression (Casu and Molynuex, 2003; Weill, 2003; Ariff and Can, 2008). The author prefers to use Tobit regression because it is more appropriate when the dependent variable is set within certain limits, which is the case with efficiency scores derived from DEA bounded between zero and one (Lovell et al., 1995; Garza-Garcia, 2012).

Data description

The banking data used in this study consist of annual figures from 101 banks between 2003 and 2011. Three different ownerships of banks are included: 5 SOCBs, 12 JSCBs, and 84 CCBs. There are gaps in the data as a result of some banks not having the necessary information for all years. So, the author opted for an unbalanced panel so as not to lose the degree of freedom. Bank-specific determinants are from the BankScope database. The two other databases used to retrieve data for industry-specific and macroeconomic determinants are: (1) the China Banking Regulatory Commission and (2) the World Bank Database. Table 4.1 shows profitability indicators; the bank-specific, industry-specific, and

Table 4.1 Variables used to estimate the determinants of bank profitability and their expected effects

Variables	**Notation**	**Measurement**	**Expected effect**	**Source**
		Dependent variables		
Return on assets	ROA	Net income/total assets		BankScope
Return on equity	ROE	Net income/shareholder equity		BankScope
Net interest margin	NIM	Net interest income/ interest earning assets		BankScope
Profit margin	PBT	Bank's earnings before tax/total assets		BankScope
		Bank-specific variables		
Bank size	LNTA	Natural logarithm of total assets	?	BankScope
Liquidity	TLTA	Total loans/total assets	?	BankScope
Capitalization	ETA	Shareholders' equity/ total assets	?	BankScope
Risk	LLPTL	Loan loss provision over total loans	+	BankScope
	Z-score	$(ROA + E/A)/\sigma(ROA)$		
	SI	Stability inefficiency		
Overhead cost	OETA	Overhead expenses/total assets	?	BankScope
Non-traditional activity	NIIGR	Non-interest income/ gross revenue	?	BankScope
Labour productivity	GRNE	Gross revenue/number of employees	+	BankScope

Table 4.1 Variables used to estimate the determinants of bank profitability and their expected effects (*cont.*)

Variables	Notation	Measurement	Expected effect	Source
Industry-specific variables				
Banking sector concentration	B(3)	Total assets of largest three banks/total assets of banking industry	?	CBRC
Banking sector development	BSD	Banking sector assets/ GDP	–	World Bank
Stock market development	SMD	Market capitalization of listed companies/GDP	+	World Bank
Macroeconomic variables				
Inflation	IR	Annual inflation rate	+	World Bank
GDP growth rate	GDPG	Annual GDP growth rate	–	World Bank

+, –, positive and negative effect, respectively. ? = no *a priori* expectation

macroeconomic determinants of bank profitability; their notation, measurements, and expected effects; and data source. Table 4.2 shows measurements of efficiency and productivity; the notation, measurements, and expected effects of potential determinants; and the data source.

Table 4.3 shows conditions for the profitability of Chinese banks between 2003 and 2011. Furthermore, the profitability of three different groups of Chinese banks is also presented. The table shows that, over the whole examined period, SOCBs had the highest profitability in terms of ROA and ROE, while the NIM of CCBs was higher than JSCBs and SOCBs. As for PBT, the profitability of SOCBs and CCBs was about the same, while the profitability of JSCBs was the lowest. The higher profitability in terms of ROA and ROE in SOCBs can be

Table 4.2 Variables used to examine the determinants of bank efficiency/productivity and their expected effects

Variables	Notation	Measurement	Expected effect	Source
		Dependent variable		
Technical efficiency	TE	Efficiency derived from DEA		BankScope
Total factor productivity	TFP	Productivity derived from DEA		BankScope
		Bank-specific variables		
Bank size	LNTA	Natural logarithm of total assets	+	BankScope
Liquidity	TLTA	Total loans/total assets	–	BankScope
Capitalization	ETA	Shareholder equity/total assets	?	BankScope
Risk	LLPTL	Loan loss provision over total loans	-	BankScope
	Z-score	$(ROA + E/A)/\sigma(ROA)$		
	SI	Stability inefficiency		
Overhead cost	OETA	Overhead expenses/total assets	–	BankScope
Non-traditional activity	NIIGR	Non-interest income/gross revenue	?	BankScope
Labour productivity	GRNE	Gross revenue/number of employees	+	BankScope

largely attributed to the overall income generated by SOCBs being higher indicating that SOCBs had advantages when engaging in both traditional and non-traditional activities. Whereas the higher NIM for CCBs suggests that their business focussed on traditional deposit–loan services. The

Table 4.2 Variables used to examine the determinants of bank efficiency/productivity and their expected effects (*cont.*)

Variables	Notation	Measurement	Expected effect	Source
		Industry-specific variables		
Banking sector concentration	B(3)	Total assets of largest three banks/total assets of banking industry	–	CBRC
Banking sector development	BSD	Banking sector assets/GDP	–	World Bank
Stock market development	SMD	Market capitalization of listed companies/GDP	—	World Bank
		Macroeconomic variables		
Inflation	IR	Annual inflation rate	–	World Bank
GDP growth rate	GDPG	Annual GDP growth rate	+	World Bank

+, –, positive and negative effect, respectively. ? = no *a priori* expectation

reason the profitability of JSCBs was the lowest is likely because they had no government support and because the higher competition between JSCBs induced managers to take higher risk, the resulting increase in the cost of monitoring risk led to a decline in bank profitability.

Panel A of Table 4.4 presents the summary statistics of explanatory variables for all Chinese banks, while Panels B, C, and D present the summary statistics of explanatory variables for SOCBs, JSCBs, and CCBs, respectively. The table shows that Chinese SOCBs were the largest in terms of total assets, while CCBs were the most liquid. This finding indicates that the loan exposure of CCBs was lower, which was attributed to the granting of loans mainly to small enterprises where the demand for funds was much smaller than in medium-sized or large enterprises. Furthermore,

Table 4.3 Descriptive statistics for profitability measures (ROA, ROE, NIM, and PBT) by ownership type

Panel A: all banks	**ROA**	**ROE**	**NIM**	**PBT**
Observations	667	661	633	644
Mean	0.008	0.12	3.008	0.012
Min	–0.04	–14.52	0.42	–0.015
Max	0.089	0.58	8.99	0.035
SD	0.006	0.58	1.14	0.0062
Panel B: SOCBs				
Observations	46	46	46	46
Mean	0.0082	0.14	2.57	0.013
Min	0.0002	–0.06	1.05	0.002
Max	0.014	0.251	3.29	0.02
SD	0.0036	0.076	0.45	0.0049
Panel C: JSCBs				
Observations	110	104	108	112
Mean	0.0054	–0.017	2.43	0.0098
Min	–0.04	–14.52	0.68	–0.015
Max	0.0133	0.3	3.42	0.019
SD	0.0058	1.443	0.51	0.005
Panel D: CCBs				
Observations	511	511	479	486
Mean	0.0073	0.13	3.18	0.013
Min	–0.005	–0.14	0.42	–0.0009
Max	0.089	0.58	8.99	0.04
SD	0.0061	0.083	1.24	0.0064

CCBs had the highest capital levels, followed by JSCBs, while the capitalization of SOCBs was the lowest. The lower liquidity of SOCBs shows that banking loans, an important factor of liabilities, accounted for a large proportion of the assets of SOCBs. The lower capitalization of SOCBs can also be explained by government injections of capital for free when necessary. The highest capital level of CCBs can be attributed to the consideration to reduce risk and further improve its stability. The statistics show that the volume of non-traditional business engaged in by SOCBs was higher than that of JSCBs and CCBs, while JSCBs had the highest labour productivity. The lower labour productivity of SOCBs than JSCBs was attributed to SOCBs being very big and difficult to manage. The lower labour productivity of CCBs can be attributed to local government being the main shareholder of banks. Government support was supposed to have a negative impact on the working practices of staff, which led to lower labour productivity The overhead cost of the three different groups of Chinese banks was much the same.

As far as the industrial and macroeconomic environment in China is concerned, the table suggests that banking sector development, inflation, and GDP growth were more stable than stock market development between 2003 and 2011. The higher volatility of the Chinese stock market can mainly be attributed to the share segregation reform initiated by the Chinese government in 2005, which led to many companies being listed on stock exchanges. By the end of 2007, there were 1,550 listed companies on the Shanghai and Hong Kong stock exchanges, the value of which reached RMB32.71 billion, accounting for 132.6 per cent of the same year's GDP. It should be remembered that stock market development was in its formative stages before 2005.

Figure 4.3a shows the profitability of SOCBs, JSCBs, and CCBs between 2003 and 2011 with profitability measured by

Table 4.4 Summary statistics: explanatory variables

	Bank size	Risk (LLPTL)	Risk (Z-score)	Risk (SI)	Liquidity	Capital	NTA	Overhead cost	Labour	C(3)	Bank	Stock	inflation	GDP growth rate
Panel A: All banks														
Observations	678	624	667	900	678	678	663	623	386	898	900	927	928	900
Mean	4.768	0.0092	1,387.6	0.325	51.5	5.44	13.5	0.011	0.0096	15.35	2.13	71.66	2.9	10.74
Min	0.71	−0.0019	−2,956.25	0.025	17.97	-14	−12.94	0.0045	0.000003	10.19	1.98	24.31	−0.77	9.1
Max	7.19	0.042	18,765	0.789	77.58	31	79.4	0.04	0.03	18.56	2.4	184.1	5.86	14.2
SD	0.938	0.0063	1,857.5	0.231	9.7	2.7	13.26	0.0037	0.0052	2.3	0.17	46.81	−0.77	1.609
Panel B: SOCBs														
Observations	46	46	46		46	46	46	46	45					
Mean	6.73	0.0064	1,252.47		51.77	4.27	16.4	0.011	0.0068					
Min	5.97	0.0021	−1,689.29		43	−14	5.4	0.0087	0.0013					
Max	7.19	0.013	5,570.4		64	7.75	43.3	0.014	0.014					
SD	0.283	0.0028	2,950.94		5.56	4.63	8.1	0.0014	0.0031					

Panel C: JSCBs														
Observations	112	107	112		112	112	110	110	89					
Mean	5.65	0.0069	809.56		55.65	4.43	10.63	0.01	0.013					
Min	4.01	0.0004	0.896		32.5	−1	−12.94	0.0054	0.003					
Max	7.19	0.025	7746.5		68.4	31	40.7	0.02	0.03					
SD	0.529	0.0038	536.37		7.1	3.35	7.63	0.002	0.0045					
Panel D: CCBs														
Observations	520	471	509		520	520	507	467	252					
Mean	4.4	0.0092	1,154.71		50.59	5.76	13.8	0.011	0.0087					
Min	0.71	−0.0019	−2,956.25		17.97	−6.42	−5.64	0.0045	0.000003					
Max	5.98	0.042	18,765		77.58	16.03	79.4	0.04	0.028					
SD	0.661	0.0069	611.45		10.24	2.48	14.46	0.004	0.005					

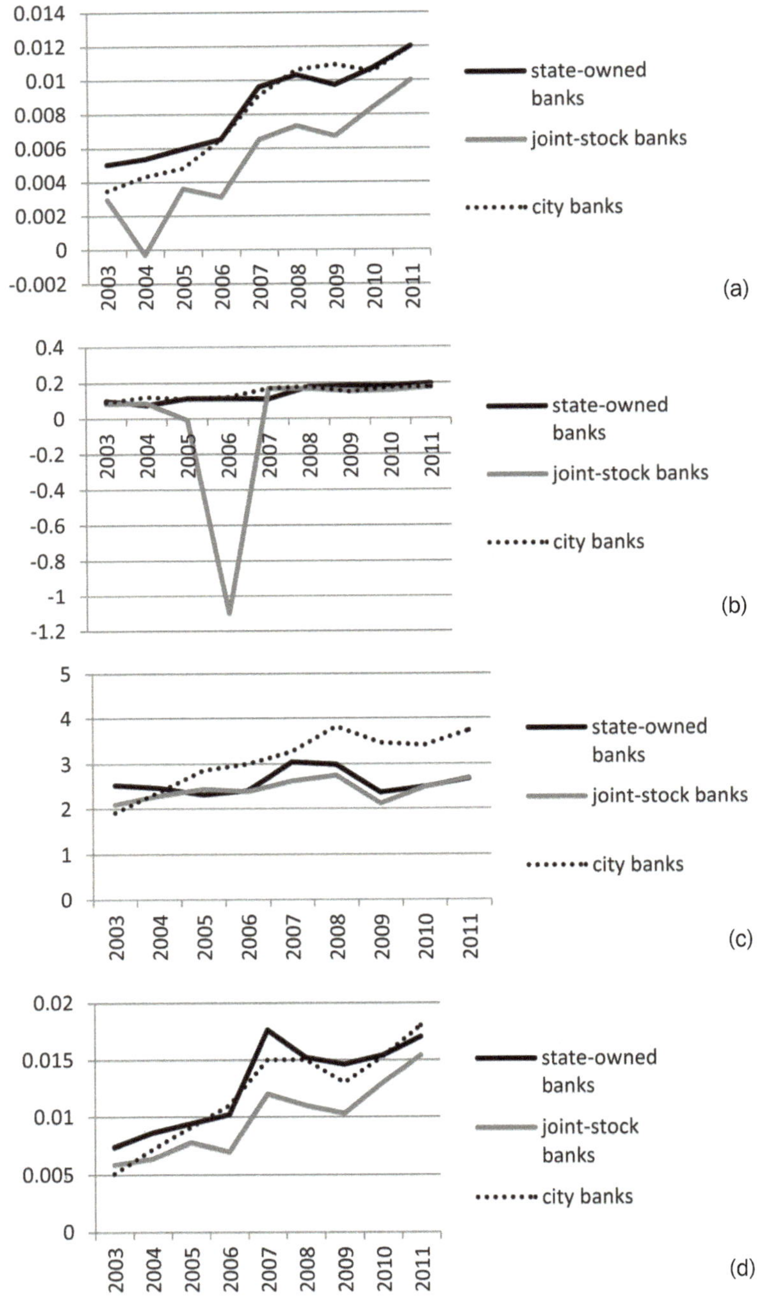

Figure 4.3 **Profitability of Chinese banks over the period 2003–11**

ROA. In general, the profitability of JSCBs was lowest and the difference in profitability between CCBs and SOCBs was small. The reason JSCBs were the least profitable can possibly be attributed to stronger competition within this banking group. JSCBs mainly served small and medium-sized enterprises, which outnumbered large enterprises, which were mainly served by SOCBs. In order to engage in a larger number of transactions, JSCBs were expected to take higher risks even without a strict risk-monitoring and management system, the higher risk leading to an increase in bank costs and a reduction in bank profitability.

Another measure of profitability is return on equity (ROE). Figure 4.3b shows the profitability (ROE) of three different groups of Chinese banks between 2003 and 2011. The results suggest that SOCBs and CCBs in China were equally profitable while the profitability of JSCBs suffered from strong volatility. The stronger volatility of ROE among JSCBs stood out in 2006, which was the only year with a negative figure. This can largely be attributed to the performance of China Everbright Bank, a major JSCB. By the end of 2006, the volume of non-performing loans in JSCBs reached RMB26.71 billion. China Everbright Bank is arguably the most important of the 12 JSCBs and has the highest volume of non-performing loans. The non-performing loan ratio for China Everbright Bank was 7.58 per cent, higher than the average level by 4.58 per cent. The large volume of non-performing loans led to a negative ROE figure.

Figure 4.3c shows that the net interest margin (NIM) of CCBs was the highest between 2004 and 2011, while the NIM of SOCBs was slightly higher than JSCBs in general. As discussed earlier, the reason CCBs had the highest NIM was their smaller scale and shorter history. Their core business was to attract deposits and make loans to small enterprises. In other words, their activities mainly focussed on interest-generating business, while the stronger competition between JSCBs induced them to engage in both traditional loan–deposit services and non-traditional activities. Furthermore, compared with SOCBs, which mainly served the large state-owned enterprises around the country, the loan demand on JSCBs was lower. Hence, the interest-generating income of JSCBs was lower than that of SOCBs.

When measured by profit margin (PBT), the profitability of SOCBs was higher than that of CCBs in general, while JSCBs had the lowest profitability (Figure 4.3d). This indicator was similar to ROA. The only difference between ROA and PBT is that the latter considers the ability of a bank to generate earnings before contractual obligations are paid (i.e., taxes paid by commercial banks). Since similar findings were reported in terms of profitability between ROA and PBT, it appears that tax had little effect on bank profitability in China in general.

Figures 4.4a–c show the conditions of risk for Chinese banks between 2003 and 2011 as measured by the ratio of loan loss provision over total loans (LLPTL), the Z-score, and stability inefficiency, respectively. Figure 4.4a shows that the volume of loan loss provision was highest in CCBs after 2004. There are a couple of reasons for this finding: (1) compared with SOCBs and JSCBs, CCBs had a shorter history and they lacked the ability to risk-manage; (2) CCBs normally made loans to small local enterprises, but they had a higher probability of default on loans. It is further shown that JSCBs generally had higher risk than SOCBs because the stronger competition between JSCBs induced bank managers to take greater risks.

The Z-score, another risk indicator, shows that in general JSCBs had a higher risk than SOCBs, while CCBs had the lowest risk (Figure 4.4b). Compared with the LLPTL, which focusses on credit risk, the Z-score is an indicator of insolvency risk. As indicated by the formula presented in the "Methodology of estimating the impact risk has on bank efficiency/

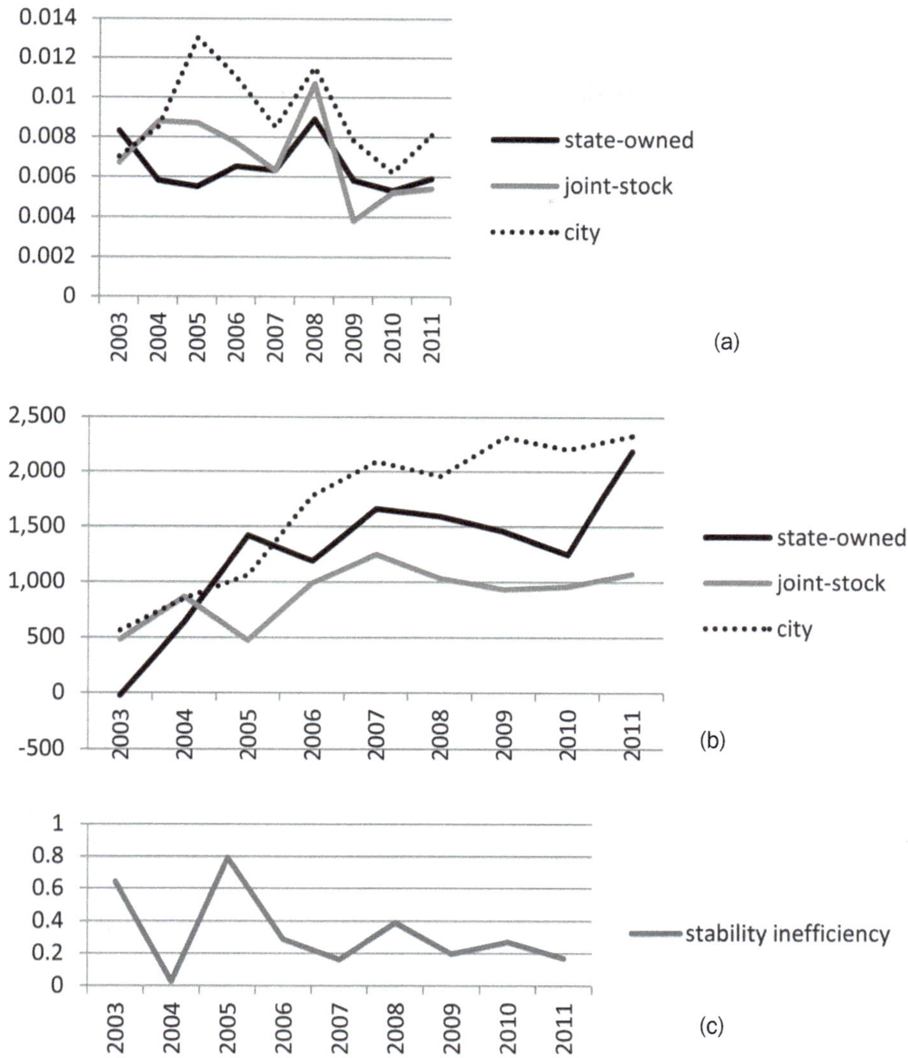

Figure 4.4 **Conditions for risk in Chinese banking industry 2003–11**

Risk measured by (a) LLPTL; (b) Z-score; and (c) stability inefficiency

productivity in China" subsection. A lower volatility of return is indicated by an increase in the Z-score (i.e., lower risk). Return in the banking sector can basically be broken down into two parts: the income derived from traditional loan–deposit business and earnings from non-traditional activity. The reason the volatility of return of CCBs is the lowest is they mainly engage in traditional loan–deposit services. The lower or no exposure to non-traditional activity reduces the volatility of return because banks lack experience and skills in these transactions, while the lower volatility of return of SOCBs can possibly be explained by the fact that they have more experience in engaging in traditional loan–deposit services and non-traditional activities than JSCBs and CCBs.

The conditions for risk in Chinese banking are examined yearly, which is reflected by stability inefficiency in Figure 4.4c. The figure shows that the conditions for risk in the Chinese banking sector over the period 2003–06 were strongly volatile, while during 2007–11 the risk was relatively more stable. The stronger volatility between 2003 and 2006 can be explained by the large volume of non-performing loans in SOCBs. The Chinese government took a number of measures to deal with these issues such as capital injection and using four asset management companies to write off non-performing loans. The relatively more stable banking sector in China between 2007 and 2011 can be attributed to two factors. (1) The financial crisis that began in 2007 made bank managers and regulatory authorities much more wary about risk-taking behaviour. The banking regulatory authority asked commercial banks to establish a risk management and rating system to ensure bank stability. (2) The 2008 Olympic Games held in Beijing stimulated economic growth, which resulted in a reduction in the default rate of loans, while the substantial increase in the number of foreign financial institutions in China not only improved the risk management of Chinese commercial banks, but brought more experience to Chinese banks in terms of engaging in non-traditional activity, which was believed to have a positive impact on bank stability.

Empirical results on the impact risk has on performance in the Chinese banking sector

This section begins by presenting and discussing results about the impact of risk on bank profitability in China. Results about technical efficiency and productivity in the Chinese banking sector are then given. Finally, the impact of risk on technical efficiency/productivity in the Chinese banking sector are reported and explained.

The impact risk has on bank profitability

This section looks at the relationship between risk and profitability while controlling for the comprehensive bank-specific, industry-specific, and macroeconomic determinants of bank profitability that we have already referred to in this chapter.

Tables 4.5, 4.6, and 4.7 give the empirical results of using LLPTL, the Z-score, and stability inefficiency as the risk indicators, respectively. One-period lagged dependent variables are significant and positive when ROA, NIM, and PBT are used as profitability indicators. All values are below 0.6, which indicates that competition in the Chinese banking sector is not very strong. It also shows that profitability in the Chinese banking sector is persistent to a certain extent.

As far as bank-specific variables are concerned, the results show that the coefficients of bank size are significant and negative suggesting the impact bank size has on bank profitability is significant and negative. The results can be explained by large commercial banks in China (such as SOCBs) being difficult to manage, by Chinese cultural characteristics, by hierarchy being very clear in Chinese companies, by final decisions being made at the management

Table 4.5 Empirical results: the impact of risk on bank profitability in China: 2003–11 (LLPTL as the risk indicator)

Variables	ROA		ROE		NIM		PBT	
	Coefficient	**T-statistic**	**Coefficient**	**T-statistic**	**Coefficient**	**T-statistic**	**Coefficient**	**T-statistic**
Lag of dependent variable	0.18[a]	8.05	0.0002	–0.65	0.49[a]	19.15	0.49[a]	32.96
Bank-specific determinants								
Bank size	–0.0008[a]	–6.53	–0.004[a]	–2.92	–0.094[a]	–5.56	–0.001[a]	–8.06
Liquidity	–0.00007[a]	–4.10	–0.0008[a]	–2.86	0.0043[b]	2.14	0.0001[a]	7.03
Capitalization	0.0001[b]	2.35	0.001	1.10	–0.015[a]	–5.44	0.0001[a]	6.67
Risk	–0.32[a]	–12.94	0.14	0.20	26.64[a]	13.16	–0.13[a]	-5.51
Overhead cost	0.47[a]	7.75	1.55	1.51	103.91[a]	14.12	0.43[a]	12.48
Non-traditional activity	1.65e–06	0.19	–0.00003	–0.22	–0.02[a]	–16.88	0.0001[a]	4.80
Labour productivity	0.19[a]	5.46	5.75[a]	13.72	4.59	0.87	0.28[a]	14.67

Industry-specific determinants								
Banking sector concentration	0.0009[a]	7.97	0.0066[a]	12.55	0.036[a]	2.71	0.001[a]	9.02
Banking sector development	0.016[a]	7.60	0.058[a]	4.30	3.01[a]	4.98	0.014[a]	19.62
Stock market development	0.00002[a]	4.53	0.0001[a]	3.07	−0.002[b]	−2.46	9.62e−06[a]	3.79
Macroeconomic determinants								
Inflation	0.0004[a]	4.24	0.009[a]	15.56	0.13[a]	6.45	0.001[a]	21.03
GDP growth rate	−0.0005[a]	−4.45	0.006[a]	5.08	0.14[a]	4.57	0.001[a]	17.96
Constant	−0.03[a]	−7.10	0.004	0.09	−7.78[a]	−4.95	−0.04[a]	−19.16
Wald test	6,183.24[a]		9,756.61[a]		12,177.12[a]		12,480.07[a]	
Sargan test	416.30		140.56		146.02		101.67	
AR(1)	$Z = -2.84$	$P = 0.005$	$Z = -2.64$	$P = 0.008$	$Z = -2.32$	$P = 0.02$	$Z = -3.10$	$P = 0.002$
AR(2)	$Z = -0.23$	$P = 0.815$	$Z = -1.49$	$P = 0.136$	$Z = -1.56$	$P = 0.12$	$Z = 1.27$	$P = 0.204$
No. of observations	213		316		204		312	

[a], 1 per cent level of significance; [b], 5 per cent level of significance

Table 4.6 Empirical results: the impact of risk on bank profitability in China: 2003–11 (Z-score as the risk indicator)

Variables	ROA		ROE		NIM		PBT	
	Coefficient	**T-statistic**	**Coefficient**	**T-statistic**	**Coefficient**	**T-statistic**	**Coefficient**	**T-statistic**
Lag of dependent variable	0.13[a]	5.51	–0.002[a]	–10.02	0.35[a]	19.43	0.54[a]	41.65
Bank-specific determinants								
Bank size	0.0001[b]	2.23	0.001	0.80	–0.05[a]	–5.74	–0.0003[a]	–4.12
Liquidity	–0.0001[a]	–7.19	–0.0003	–1.45	0.006[a]	3.50	–7.93e–07	–0.08
Capitalization	0.0002[a]	7.08	0.004[a]	8.79	–0.01[c]	–2.59	0.0001[a]	3.31
Risk	3.80e–07[a]	–3.11	–6.14e–06[a]	-6.60	0.0001[a]	6.56	2.43e–07[a]	3.43
Overhead cost	0.26[a]	9.07	1.15	1.05	158.99[a]	23.31	0.46[a]	15.74
Non-traditional activity	–0.00004[a]	–7.31	0.0003[a]	3.60	–0.02[a]	–33.14	0.00003[a]	4.44
Labour productivity	0.07[a]	2.91	3.99[a]	14.24	13.01[a]	3.67	0.16[a]	18.67

Industry-specific determinants								
Banking sector concentration	0.0006[a]	7.07	0.008[a]	6.75	0.17[a]	15.96	0.0003[a]	6.57
Banking sector development	0.02[a]	14.91	0.071[a]	6.51	4.24[a]	13.23	0.012[a]	20.58
Stock market development	8.83e−06[a]	2.78	0.00002	0.58	−0.001[a]	−3.39	7.71e−06[a]	4.28
Macroeconomic determinants								
Inflation	0.0005[a]	7.20	0.01[a]	7.19	0.12[a]	10.55	0.0008[a]	15.90
GDP growth rate	0.00006	0.55	0.008[a]	5.96	0.07[a]	5.55	0.001[a]	23.31
Constant	−0.05[a]	−14.50	−0.06[b]	−1.98	−12.12[a]	−13.95	−0.04[a]	-32.60
Wald test	530,855[a]		376,552[a]		1.36e+06[a]		6.78e+06[a]	
Sargan test	352.25		222.42		504.96		332.57	
AR(1)	$Z = -2.66$	$P = 0.008$	$Z = -2.24$	$P = 0.025$	$Z = -1.98$	$P = 0.048$	$Z = -2.67$	$P = 0.008$
AR(2)	$Z = -0.83$	$P = 0.406$	$Z = -1.61$	$P = 0.107$	$Z = -1.10$	$P = 0.271$	$Z = 1.33$	$P = 0.182$
No. of observations	161		237		162		243	

[a], 1 per cent level of significance; [b], 5 per cent level of significance; [c], 10 per cent level of significance

Table 4.7 Empirical results: the impact of risk on bank profitability in China: 2003–11 (stability inefficiency as the risk indicator)

Variables	ROA		ROE		NIM		PBT	
	Coefficient	**T-statistic**	**Coefficient**	**T-statistic**	**Coefficient**	**T-statistic**	**Coefficient**	**T-statistic**
Lag of dependent variable	0.24[a]	6.09	–0.003[a]	–5.59	0.52[a]	24.21	0.57[a]	34.38
Bank-specific determinants								
Bank size	0.00003	0.33	–0.004[a]	–3.63	–0.082[a]	–6.05	–0.0006[a]	–10.48
Liquidity	–0.00005[a]	–3.45	–0.0008[a]	–3.38	0.007[a]	3.37	0.00006[a]	5.31
Capitalization	0.0001[b]	2.42	0.0004	0.64	0.015[a]	2.94	0.0001[a]	4.23
Risk	0.0001	0.21	0.011[a]	3.24	–0.074	–1.32	0.0006[b]	2.22
Overhead cost	0.45[a]	8.40	2.32[c]	1.85	130.77[a]	10.91	0.47[a]	8.87
Non-traditional activity	–0.00002[a]	–2.93	–0.0002	–1.19	–0.02[a]	–13.46	0.00004[a]	4.14
Labour productivity	0.17[a]	4.35	5.86[a]	11.40	4.27	0.89	0.19[a]	8.13

Industry-specific determinants								
Banking sector concentration	0.0003[b]	1.99	0.008[a]	6.93	0.12[a]	5.79	0.0003[a]	4.42
Banking sector development	0.016[a]	5.56	0.073[a]	3.33	3.73[a]	7.22	0.014[a]	15.17
Stock market development	9.24e–06[c]	1.86	0.0001[a]	3.28	–0.002[a]	–3.84	5.51e–06[a]	2.98
Macroeconomic determinants								
Inflation	0.0005[a]	4.07	0.011[a]	7.12	0.12[a]	7.91	0.0009[a]	12.01
GDP growth rate	0.0002	1.14	0.007[a]	3.87	0.12[a]	6.49	0.001[a]	14.30
Constant	–0.04[a]	–5.69	–0.02	–0.30	–10.78[a]	7.43	–0.04[a]	–17.66
Wald test	2,152.45[a]		15,944[a]		9,992[a]		38,162.4[a]	
Sargan test	453.76		322.69		832.89		508.53	
AR(1)	$Z = -2.94$	$P = 0.003$	$Z = -2.60$	$P = 0.009$	$Z = -1.97$	$P = 0.049$	$Z = -3.11$	$P = 0.002$
AR(2)	$Z = -0.21$	$P = 0.833$	$Z = -1.37$	$P = 0.172$	$Z = -1.42$	$P = 0.156$	$Z = 1.50$	$P = 0.134$
No. of observations	222		327		210		321	

[a], 1 per cent level of significance; [b], 5 per cent level of significance; [c], 10 per cent level of significance

level on a one-by-one basis, and by complicated bureaucratic procedures hindering improvements in profitability in the banking sector. In addition, the coefficients of labour productivity are significant and positive indicating the impact labour productivity has on bank profitability is significant and positive. This has relevant policy implications for bank management. Chinese banks should recruit personnel not only on the basis of educational background, but also on professional work experience. Furthermore, Chinese banks should put in place relevant policies to retain experienced staff and provide more training opportunities for new staff who have little or no working experience. In this way labour productivity can be increased and bank profitability improved. Higher overhead costs can contribute to improvements in profitability in terms of ROA, NIM, and PBT in the Chinese banking sector. This means that, as a result of the difference between loan and deposit interest rates, Chinese banks can pass overhead costs on to depositors. It also means that Chinese banks can spend more money to recruit higher quality staff with more experience and retain staff who have performed well (i.e., staff whose contribution to improvements in profitability exceeds the salaries paid to them). Furthermore, some banks advertise their banking products and services to attract more customers. The money Chinese banks spend on advertising also stimulates improvements in profitability.

Tables 4.5–4.7 show the impact risk has on bank profitability to be negligible. There are a couple of reasons for this. First, this finding can be largely explained when looked at from the perspective of SOCBs. As discussed in Chapter 2, there were three occasions when non-performing loans of SOCBs were written off by four asset management companies: 1999, 2004, and 2005. Apart from writing off non-performing loans, the government injected capital into SOCBs over the period 2003–05. The non-performing loans held by SOCBs (higher risk) did not affect their profitability because of this government support. The second reason for this finding can be explained when looked at from the perspective of CCBs. In much the same way as central government supported the operation of SOCBs, local government also invested funds to offset the large volume of non-performing loans held by CCBs. Thus, risk clearly does not affect the profitability of these banks. Liquidity is found to be significantly and positively related to the NIM of Chinese banks indicating that the higher the volumes of loans made by banks the greater the amount of net interest generated. This does not necessarily mean that Chinese banks have improved risk management as this finding can be partly attributed to economic growth in China, which has the effect of decreasing the default rate of loans. However, liquidity is significantly and negatively related to the ROA of Chinese banks. This can be explained by the larger volumes of loans granted by Chinese commercial banks being accompanied by higher amounts of expenses. For instance, in order to attract more loans, banks will spend more money on establishing relationships with different enterprises. Increases in expenses incurred are more than increases in interest income earned, which leads to a decline in ROA. Furthermore, this result probably indicates that non-traditional activity has become increasingly important in the operation of banks – the large volume of loan services provided by banks reduces non-interest income, which further leads to a decline in ROA. The capital level of Chinese banks is found to be significantly and positively related to profitability in terms of ROA and PBT, while non-traditional activity is found to be significantly and negatively related to NIM and at the same time significantly and positively related to PBT. This finding shows that engagement in non-traditional activity to some extent improves the profitability of Chinese commercial banks, while the larger volume of non-traditional activity engaged in by Chinese banks reduces the amount of traditional loan–deposit services provided, which further leads to a decline in NIM. Keeping a higher level of capital works as a cushion to absorb negative shocks, which in turn lowers the bankruptcy cost and increases bank profitability especially for medium and small-sized commercial banks (large SOCBs do not have this bankruptcy cost because they are considered too big to fail).

Turning now to industry-specific variables, the results indicate that the higher developed the banking sector the higher the profitability of Chinese banks. This result can be explained by the demand for banking services in a higher developed banking sector increasing, while a market with higher demand normally will attract more potential competitors. However, the procedure and regulations that need to be complied with for establishing a new bank in China is complicated and strict, which has the effect of increasing the profitability of existing banks. This can be further explained from the perspective of demand and supply. As discussed earlier, when the banking sector is more highly developed, the demand for banking products and services increases. While the complicated procedure of establishing new banks decreases the supply of banking products and services, the resulting increase in the price of providing banking products and services increases the income and profitability of existing banks. Stock market development is significantly and positively related to Chinese bank profitability in terms of ROA and PBT, while it is significantly and negatively related to NIM. This is attributed to a higher developed stock market generating more information about firms, which saves the cost banks would have to incur to monitor the risk and leads to higher profitability. On the other hand, higher developed stock markets increase the number of firms wanting to obtain funds from stock markets rather than banks, and the decrease in the volumes of loans reduces the NIM of Chinese banks. Banking sector concentration is found to be significantly and positively related to the profitability of Chinese banks. This suggests that the SCP hypothesis is applicable to the Chinese banking sector. This is testimony to the number of smaller banks, especially CCBs, merging in recent years to obtain higher profitability.

As far as the macroeconomic determinants of bank profitability are concerned, the results show that inflation is significantly and positively related to Chinese bank profitability indicating that the profitability of Chinese banks is higher when inflation is high. This finding can be explained by Chinese banks having the ability to anticipate inflation and being able to adjust the interest rate appropriately and promptly, which results in revenue increasing more than cost and, thus, higher profitability is achieved. The rate of growth in GDP is found to be significantly and positively related to Chinese bank profitability in terms of ROE, NIM, and PBT suggesting that the profitability of Chinese banks is higher during economic booms. This finding can be attributed to lending rates increasing and the probability of default being less during economic growth.

Estimation of technical efficiency/productivity in the Chinese banking sector

The technical efficiency of Chinese banks (2003–11)

Before obtaining the efficiency scores/productivity of Chinese banks, the inputs and outputs used to estimate technical efficiency/productivity need to be chosen. The suggestions made by Chen et al. (2005) and Fu and Heffernan (2007) are followed in terms of the selection of banking inputs and outputs. More specifically, the outputs used are total loans,

Table 4.8 Summary statistics of inputs and outputs used to estimate efficiency scores

Variables	Observations	Mean	S.D	Min	Max
Inputs					
Total expenses	616	3.29	0.84	0.18	5.57
Price of funds	616	1.25	0.18	0.74	1.96
Price of capital	616	1.93	0.26	1.24	2.83
Outputs					
Total loans	616	4.54	0.86	1.12	6.88
Securities	616	4.13	0.96	−0.405	6.6
Non-interest income	616	2.26	0.98	−2.1	5.04
Total deposits	616	4.8	0.86	1.82	7.14

securities, non-interest income, and total deposits; while the inputs include total expenses (interest and non-interest expenses), price of deposits (interest paid on deposits divided by deposits), and price of capital (non-interest expenses divided by fixed assets). Table 4.8 provides summary statistics on inputs and outputs. When it comes to banking inputs, the statistics show that total expenses between Chinese commercial banks substantially differ compared with the price of capital and price of funds reflected by standard deviation. As the size of Chinese banks differs widely (i.e., SOCBs are large while CCBs are relatively small), the volumes of traditional loan–deposit services and non-traditional activities engaged in are different, which leads to large differences in interest and non-interest expenses. As for banking outputs, greater differences can be noticed in securities and non-interest income generated by banks. This reflects major differences in Chinese commercial banks when it comes to experience and skills in engaging in non-traditional activities.

Table 4.9 Mean values of technical efficiency, pure technical efficiency, and scale efficiency of all Chinese commercial banks: 2003–11

Banks/efficiency scores	Technical efficiency	Pure technical efficiency	Scale efficiency
State-owned commercial banks	0.966	0.971	0.995
Joint stock commercial banks	0.908	0.92	0.979
City commercial banks	0.911	0.922	0.973

The overall technical efficiency scores of SOCBs, JSCBs, and CCBs are estimated using the CCR model, and then the pure technical and scale efficiency scores are derived from the BCC model. Table 4.9 and Figure 4.5 present the mean values of the technical, pure technical, and scale efficiency of the three different ownerships of banks over the period 2003–11.

The findings show that SOCBs had the highest overall technical efficiency between 2003 and 2011, followed by

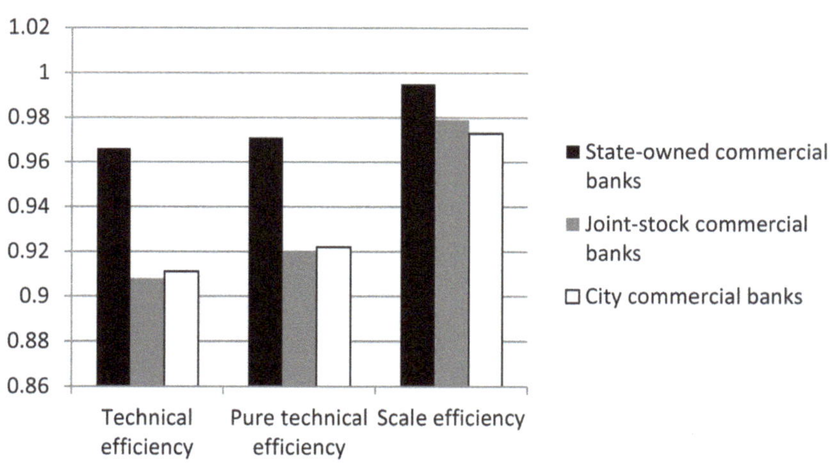

Figure 4.5 **Technical efficiency scores of state-owned, joint stock, and city banks in China (2003–11)**

CCBs, while JSCBs had the lowest technical efficiency score. The reason the technical efficiency of SOCBs was highest can be attributed to SOCBs completing their initial public offerings. The China Construction Bank listed on the Hong Kong and Shanghai stock exchanges in 2005 and 2007, respectively; the Bank of China listed on the Shanghai and Hong Kong stock exchanges in 2006; the Industrial and Commercial Bank of China listed on the Hong Kong and Shanghai stock exchanges in 2006; the Bank of Communication listed on the Hong Kong and Shanghai stock exchanges in 2005 and 2007, respectively; and the last SOCB, the Agricultural Bank of China completed its initial public offering in 2010 on the Shanghai and Hong Kong stock exchanges. The listing of these banks improved corporate governance and further increased bank efficiency.However, the difference in the efficiency scores between CCBs and JSCBs was smaller than that between SOCBs and JSCBs. The reason JSCBs had the lowest technical efficiency can be explained by the fact they mainly served small and medium-sized enterprises all over the country, easily outnumbering large state-owned enterprises. The resultant higher competition prompted bank managers to engage in both traditional loan–deposit services and non-traditional activities. As a result of there being greater competition in both these areas, JSCBs underwent higher risk, while the resulting increase in the cost of monitoring risk led to a decline in technical efficiency. The overall technical efficiency scores of SOCBs, JSCBs, and CCBs in China were 0.966, 0.908, and 0.911, respectively; these figures indicate that SOCBs were by and large relatively inefficient and could have further reduced their factors of production by 3.4 per cent by maintaining the same output level. In other words, JSCBs and CCBs in China could have further reduced their factors of production by 9.2 and 8.9 per cent, respectively.

Breaking technical efficiency down into pure technical efficiency and scale efficiency, the results show that SOCBs had the highest pure technical efficiency score, followed by CCBs, while JSCBs had the lowest pure technical efficiency score. The scale efficiency of Chinese commercial banks was higher than their pure technical efficiency. This indicates that scale efficiency contributed more than pure technical efficiency to overall efficiency in the Chinese banking industry. In other words, inefficiency in Chinese commercial banks can be attributed to pure technical inefficiency rather than scale inefficiency. The results also suggest that Chinese commercial banks were pure technical inefficient when it came to allocation of inputs and outputs in banking.

Productivity in the Chinese banking sector (2003–11)

Table 4.10 and Figure 4.6 report the productivity growth of the three different ownerships of Chinese banks between 2003 and 2011. The base year is 2003, the productivity index of which takes a value of 1. Any figure greater than 1 in subsequent years is indicative of productivity growth, while any figure lower than 1 is indicative of productivity decline. The figure and table show that the highest productivity growth and decline occurred in 2005 and 2008 for SOCBs and CCBs, respectively. The highest productivity growth of SOCBs in 2005 can be attributed to two banks listing on the stock exchanges: the China Construction Bank and the Bank of Communication. The strongest decline in the productivity in CCBs in 2008 can be explained by most CCBs being the main financial institutions serving small local enterprises, while since 2008 the trend for CCBs was to extend their business to other cities. The resultant stronger competition reduced bank outputs and led to a decline in productivity. In 2005 all ownerships of Chinese commercial banks experienced productivity growth, followed in short order by productivity

Table 4.10 The Malmquist productivity index of Chinese state-owned, joint stock, and city commercial banks: 2003–11

Year/banks	State owned	Joint stock	City
2003	1.000	1.000	1.000
2004	1.00275	0.9897	0.9846
2005	1.1095	1.0334	1.0379
2006	0.9958	0.973	0.9705
2007	0.9545	0.9989	1.0312
2008	0.9682	0.9789	0.9386
2009	1.0648	1.0476	1.0583
2010	0.960	0.974	0.997
2011	0.934	0.971	0.998

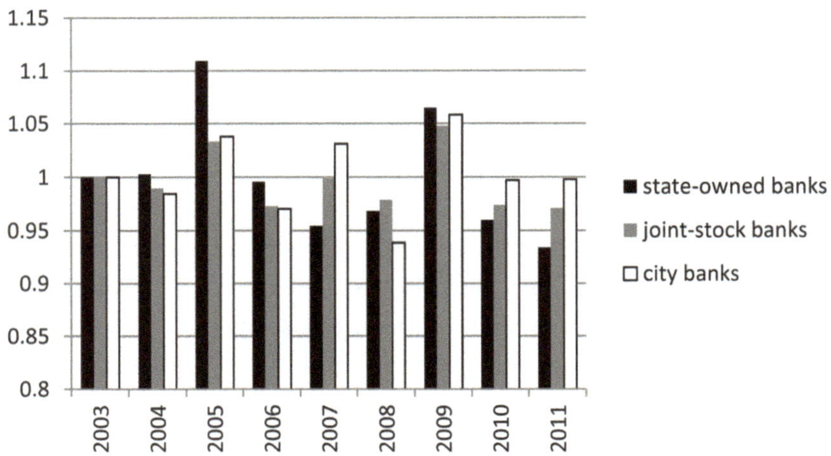

Figure 4.6 **Productivity growth of the three ownerships of Chinese banks over the period 2003–11**

decline in 2006. The productivity decline of all ownerships of commercial banks can possibly be attributed to stronger competition between foreign banks and domestic commercial banks as a result of the restrictions on the services provided by foreign banks having been removed by 2006. CCBs were the only bank group to experience productivity improvement in 2007. This finding can partly be explained by three CCBs – the Bank of Beijing, the Bank of Nanjing, and the Bank of Ningbo – successfully getting listed on the Shanghai and Shenzhen stock exchanges. By contrast, all bank groups experienced productivity decline between 2008 and 2011, although 2009 was an exception. The productivity decline in 2008 can be attributed to the global financial crisis having a negative impact on the Chinese banking sector. Productivity growth for all three groups of bank can possibly be explained by the higher loan exposure of the banking industry. According to the 2008 and 2009 annual reports of the CBRC, liquidity in the Chinese banking sector at the end of 2009 was 46.4 per cent, much lower than the ratio in 2008 when the figure was 50.07 per cent; the higher the number of loans made by banks the greater the increase in productivity. The productivity decline in 2010 and 2011 can be attributed to higher cost of funds. According to data from the World Bank, the deposit interest rates in 2010 and 2011 were 3.5 and 3.0 per cent, higher than previous years; the higher the input price the lower the bank productivity.

The impact risk has on technical efficiency in the Chinese banking sector

Tables 4.11–4.13 report empirical results about the impact risk has on technical efficiency in the Chinese banking sector while controlling for comprehensive bank-specific, industry-specific, and macroeconomic determinants of bank efficiency. A

Table 4.11 The impact of risk on efficiency (loan loss provisions over total loans as the risk indicator)

Variables	Technical efficiency		Pure technical efficiency		Scale efficiency	
	Coefficient	T-statistic	Coefficient	T-statistic	Coefficient	T-statistic
Bank-specific determinants						
Bank size	0.0084	1.38	0.008	1.44	0.002	0.40
Liquidity	–0.0008[c]	–1.84	–0.0007	–1.65	0.0003	0.51
Capitalization	–0.0003	–0.36	–0.00005	–0.05	–0.002	–1.36
Risk	–0.18	–0.41	–0.44	–1.07	1.12	1.56
Overhead cost	–1.36	–0.98	–2.47[c]	–1.91	–3.27	–1.61
Non-traditional activity	0.004	1.35	0.0004[c]	1.84	0.0006	1.39
Labour productivity	–3.63[a]	–4.45	4.01[a]	–5.21	–1.56	–1.39
Industry-specific variables						
Banking sector concentration	0.02[a]	5.44	0.02[a]	5.61	0.01[c]	1.78
Banking sector development	0.18[a]	5.57	0.194[a]	6.46	0.032	0.61
Stock market development	0.0001	1.37	0.0001	1.16	0.0001	0.71

Macroeconomic variables						
Inflation	–0.006[b]	–1.96	–0.005[c]	–1.77	–0.002	–0.32
GDP growth rate	–0.009[b]	–2.31	–0.008[b]	–2.26	–0.006	–0.89
Constant	0.43[a]	5.28	0.42[a]	5.61	0.84[a]	6.53
Number of observations	312		313		313	
Wald chi square	458.30[a]		522.63[a]		32.59[a]	
Log likelihood	429.76		431.29		286.17	

[a], 1 per cent level of significance; [b], 5 per cent level of significance; [c], 10 per cent level of significance

Table 4.12 The impact of risk on efficiency (Z-score as the risk indicator)

Variables	Technical efficiency		Pure technical efficiency		Scale efficiency	
	Coefficient	T-statistic	Coefficient	T-statistic	Coefficient	T-statistic
Bank-specific determinants						
Bank size	0.012[c]	1.81	0.014[b]	2.22	−0.0007	−0.09
Liquidity	−0.001	−1.52	−0.0005	−0.93	0.0003	0.30
Capitalization	−0.002	−1.27	−0.0002	−0.18	−0.003	−1.07
Risk	4.07e−06	1.56	2.11e−06	0.90	−2.02e−06	−0.44
Overhead cost	−3.34[b]	−2.16	−3.99[a]	−2.87	−4.43[c]	−1.67
Non-traditional activity	0.0002	0.77	0.0002	0.79	0.001[c]	1.66
Labour productivity	−3.94[a]	−4.25	−3.91[a]	−4.72	−2.09	−1.43
Industry-specific variables						
Banking sector concentration	0.017[a]	4.94	0.02[a]	5.36	0.01	1.43
Banking sector development	0.17[a]	4.56	0.17[a]	5.18	0.03	0.40
Stock market development	0.0001	1.15	0.0001	1.42	0.0001	0.36

Macroeconomic variables						
Inflation	−0.006[c]	−1.70	−0.006[c]	−1.86	−0.001	−0.17
GDP growth rate	−0.009[b]	−2.16	−0.009[b]	−2.40	−0.006	−0.70
Constant	0.46[a]	5.12	0.44[a]	5.48	0.901[a]	5.33
Number of observations	236		237		237	
Wald chi square	354.74[a]		412.93[a]		26.51[a]	
Log likelihood	325.3		331.06		192.36	

[a], 1 per cent level of significance; [b], 5 per cent level of significance; [c], 10 per cent level of significance

Table 4.13 The impact of risk on efficiency (stability inefficiency as the risk indicator)

Variables	Technical efficiency		Pure technical efficiency		Scale efficiency	
	Coefficient	T-statistic	Coefficient	T-statistic	Coefficient	T-statistic
Bank-specific determinants						
Bank size	0.008	1.28	0.0086	1.51	–0.001	–0.17
Liquidity	–0.0007[c]	–1.74	–0.0007[c]	–1.70	0.0002	0.26
Capitalization	0.0004	–0.36	–0.0001	–0.09	–0.002	–1.33
Risk	–0.024	–1.58	–0.025[c]	–1.84	–0.028	–1.02
Overhead cost	–2.41[c]	–1.81	–3.24[a]	–2.64	–2.8	–1.41
Non-traditional activity	0.0004[c]	1.75	0.0005[b]	2.22	0.0007	1.64
Labour productivity	–3.7[a]	–4.65	–4.1[a]	–5.45	–1.38	–1.25
Industry-specific variables						
Banking sector concentration	0.019[a]	5.19	0.019[a]	5.56	0.014[b]	2.08
Banking sector development	0.156[a]	3.89	0.164[a]	4.48	–0.021	–0.31
Stock market development	0.0002	1.61	0.0002	1.63	0.0002	0.97

Macroeconomic variables						
Inflation	−0.009[b]	−2.27	−0.009	−2.39	−0.007	−0.90
GDP growth rate	−0.011[c]	−2.57	−0.011[a]	−2.77	−0.01	−1.36
Constant	0.49[a]	5.20	0.48[a]	5.67	0.997[a]	6.30
Number of observations	320		321		321	
Wald chi square	495.9[a]		556.44[a]		33.14[a]	
Log likelihood	437.7		439.58		290.81	

[a], 1 per cent level of significance; [b], 5 per cent level of significance; [c], 10 per cent level of significance

comparison of the three tables indicates that overhead cost is significantly and negatively related to the pure technical efficiency of Chinese banks suggesting that Chinese bank with higher overhead costs normally have lower pure technical efficiency. Pure technical efficiency reflects the managerial performance of banks at organizing and allocating inputs in the production process. Chinese banks with higher overhead costs point to a failure of the bank to manage resources well. Waste and inappropriate use of inputs to produce a certain number of outputs leads to a decline in pure technical efficiency. Labour productivity is another bank-specific determinant that is found to be significantly and negatively related to the technical efficiency of Chinese banks indicating that Chinese banks with higher labour productivity normally have lower technical efficiency. This result can be explained by banks normally paying higher salaries in order to recruit and retain experienced and more productive staff; the resultant increase in the price of labour reduces the technical efficiency of banks. The impact risk has on efficiency in the Chinese banking sector appears to be negligible.

As for the industry-specific determinants of bank efficiency, the findings suggest that banking sector concentration is significantly and positively related to the technical and pure technical efficiency of Chinese banks underlining the fact that Chinese banks in a more concentrated banking market normally have higher technical and pure technical efficiency. When the banking market is more concentrated CCBs are more likely to merge, the purpose of which is to maximize profits by better allocation of resources, such as getting rid of redundant staff, integrating resources, making better use of technology and managerial skills. A series of strategies should be employed to reduce the number of inputs used to produce a certain number of outputs, and in so doing bring about higher technical and pure technical efficiency. It is further reported that banking sector development is significantly and positively related to the technical and pure technical efficiency of Chinese banking indicating that the technical and pure technical efficiency of Chinese banks is higher in a more developed banking sector. Such a banking sector plays a major role in the economy and brings about an increase in the demand for banking services. When there is an increased demand for banking services, the number of traditional deposit–loan services and non-traditional business activities engaged in by Chinese banks proliferates. Any increase in outputs leads to an improvement in efficiency.

As far as macroeconomic determinants are concerned, it is reported that inflation is significantly and negatively related to the technical efficiency of Chinese banking suggesting that the technical efficiency of Chinese banking is higher when inflation is lower. When inflation is high, bank-lending activities decrease. As loans are outputs in banking production, any decrease in their number reduces output production and leads to a decline in the technical efficiency of Chinese banks. The GDP growth rate is found to be significantly and negatively related to the technical and pure technical efficiency of Chinese banks suggesting that the technical and pure technical efficiency of Chinese banks is lower during economic booms. This finding can be explained by economic activity increasing during booms with banks engaging in more business. To deal with such an increase in transactions, banks spend more money on fixed assets, funds, and labour. The negative impact GDP has on bank efficiency in China indicates that increases in the input cost are greater than those in output production.

As for the impact risk had on Chinese bank productivity between 2003 and 2011, Table 4.14 reports robustness results using three different risk indicators. The results suggest that banking sector concentration was significantly and negatively related to productivity in Chinese banks

Table 4.14 The impact of risk on productivity in Chinese banking sector

Variables	Risk = ratio of loan loss provisions over total loans (LLPTL)		Risk = Z-score		Risk = stability inefficiency	
	Coefficient	**T-statistic**	**Coefficient**	**T-statistic**	**Coefficient**	**T-statistic**
Bank-specific determinants						
Bank size	0.016	1.18	0.031[c]	1.68	0.017	1.26
Liquidity	–0.0004	–0.16	–0.0003	–0.10	–0.001	–0.44
Capitalization	0.002	0.32	–0.005	–0.62	0.0009	0.18
Risk (LLPTL)	–1.61	–0.56				
Risk (Z-score)			0.00002	1.31		
Risk (stability inefficiency)					0.088	0.46
Overhead cost	1.67	0.18	–5.03	–0.49	3.15	0.38
Non-traditional activity	–0.001	–0.72	0.001	0.73	–0.001	–0.73
Labour productivity	–3.38	–0.95	0.53	0.13	–2.5	–0.75

Industry-specific variables						
Banking sector concentration	−0.056[b]	−2.11	−0.07[b]	−2.21	−0.07[c]	−1.78
Banking sector development	2.64[a]	2.73	3.21[a]	2.94	1.51	0.59
Stock market development	−0.005[a]	−2.93	−0.007[a]	−3.27	−0.003	−0.81
Macroeconomic variables						
Inflation	0.108[b]	2.52	0.14[a]	2.76	0.075	0.96
GDP growth rate	0.19[a]	2.94	0.24[a]	3.28	0.14	1.06
Constant	−5.69[b]	−2.27	−7.32[c]	−2.58	−2.66	−0.39
Number of observations	98		86		99	
Wald chi square	29.43[a]		26.56[a]		29.82	
Log likelihood	22.69		22.69		24.2	

[a], 1 per cent level of significance; [b], 5 per cent level of significance; [c], 10 per cent level of significance

indicating that the productivity of Chinese banks was relatively higher when the banking market became more concentrated.

Summary and conclusion

According to statistics from the World Bank, the domestic credit provided by the banking sector at the end of 2010 accounted for 146.3 per cent of GDP, higher than the figures in 2008 and 2009 (120.8 and 145.1 per cent, respectively). This statistic shows that the Chinese banking sector plays an increasingly important role in the economy. The importance of the banking sector is emphasized by bank managers, the banking regulatory authority, and the government. The large volume of non-performing loans, especially those held by SOCBs, made improvements in the performance of the Chinese banking industry more difficult. As a consequence of the Asian financial crisis in 2007, banking sector stability and reduction of risk-taking behaviour in the Chinese banking sector became priority tasks to be achieved.

This chapter looks at the performance of the Chinese banking sector over the period 2003–11 from different perspectives. More specifically, the profitability and efficiency/productivity of Chinese banks are evaluated. Four profitability indicators are used to measure Chinese bank profitability: ROA, ROE, NIM, and PBT. Apart from analysing and comparing the profitability of the three different ownerships of banks, the impact risk has on bank profitability in China is also examined while controlling for comprehensive bank-specific, industry-specific, and macroeconomic determinants of bank profitability. The results suggest that risk has a negligible impact on Chinese bank profitability. This finding shows that, despite SOCBs having a large number of non-performing loans, higher profitability can still be achieved because of the measures taken by the Chinese government to protect and support the operation of SOCBs including capital injection and writing off non-performing loans through the services of four asset management companies. The results suggest the determinants of bank profitability in China are: (1) Chinese banks with larger total assets normally have lower profitability; (2) Chinese banks whose staff are more productive normally have higher profitability; (3) a more developed banking sector contributes to improvements in the profitability of Chinese banks; (4) the profitability of Chinese banks is higher in a more concentrated banking market; and (5) inflation has a significant and positive impact on Chinese bank profitability.

Apart from looking at bank profitability, the technical efficiency of Chinese banks is also evaluated. The results indicate that SOCBs had the highest technical efficiency between 2003 and 2011, followed by CCBs, while the technical efficiency of JSCBs was the lowest. The finding further reports that scale efficiency contributed more to the overall technical efficiency of Chinese banks, and that Chinese banks over the study period were pure technical inefficient. In other words, they misallocated input and output in banking operation. In the latter part of this chapter's analysis, the determinants of technical efficiency in the Chinese banking sector are assessed with a special focus on the impact risk has on technical efficiency. The results indicate that Chinese banks with higher overhead costs normally have lower pure technical efficiency indicating that higher overhead costs are reflective of bank managers lacking the skills to manage input resources appropriately. Furthermore, the productivity of labour was found to be significantly and negatively related to the technical efficiency of Chinese banks. As far as the industry-specific determinants of technical efficiency are concerned, the findings suggest that in a more concentrated and developed banking market, the technical and pure technical efficiencies of Chinese banks are higher. In other words, bank managers are better able to allocate resources in highly concentrated and developed banking markets. As for the macroeconomic environment, the findings suggest that higher inflation leads to a decline in the technical efficiency of Chinese banks, while it will be improved during periods of economic downturn.

Finally, the productivity of the three different ownerships of Chinese banks is examined. Using 2003 as the reference year, the results of comparing the productivity index of SOCBs, JSCBs, and CCBs from 2004 to 2011 indicate that SOCBs had the highest productivity growth in 2005 while CCBs had the highest productivity decline in 2007. Furthermore, all commercial banks experienced productivity growth in 2005 and productivity decline in 2006. Between 2008 and 2011, all banks experienced productivity decline except in 2009.

By analysing bank profitability, technical efficiency, and productivity, the study provides valuable policy implications for bank managers, the regulatory authority, and the government about how to improve the performance of the Chinese banking sector: (1) Bank managers should make greater efforts to recruit staff who are more experienced and provide more training and opportunities for existing staff to improve productivity. Furthermore, there should be relevant policies on retaining experienced staff such as increasing salaries and introducing bonus schemes. (2) There should be relevant monetary policies preventing GDP from undergoing high-speed growth, while inflation should be carefully controlled to counterbalance increases in profitability and decreases in bank efficiency. (3) The Chinese government should continue to encourage large SOCBs to engage in more traditional loan–deposit services and non-traditional activities, with the aim of increasing the total assets of China's large banks and helping the Chinese banking sector improve profitability and technical efficiency.

Notes

1. The section entitled "Methodology and data investigating the impact risk has on bank performance in China" gives information on how the Z-score and stability inefficiency are measured.
2. The Big 4 state-owned banks are the Bank of China (BOC), the China Construction Bank (CCB), the Agricultural Bank of China (ABC), and the Industrial and Commercial Bank of China (ICBC).
3. The translog specification is a commonly used generalization of the Cobb–Douglas function.
4. A unit root is a feature of processes evolving through time and causing problems in statistical inference involving time series models.

5

Competition in the Chinese banking sector

Abstract: In the previous chapter the author investigated bank performance with special emphasis on the impact risk has on bank performance in the Chinese banking sector. Apart from bank performance, the Chinese government and the banking regulatory authority attached importance to increasing competitive conditions in the Chinese banking sector and by so doing improve bank performance. In this chapter the author examines the competitive conditions in the Chinese banking sector between 2003 and 2011. Furthermore, the author looks at the impact competition has had on the risk-taking behaviour of Chinese banks.

This chapter is structured as follows: the first section is entitled "Theory of bank competition" and looks at the various factors involved. This is followed by "Methodology behind estimating bank competition" and looks at econometric methods to test the impact of bank competition on bank risk. "Literature review" looks at the empirical literature on bank competition in China and empirical research into the impact competition has on bank risk. There then follows a section "Empirical results", which looks at bank competition and the impact bank competition has on bank risk in China. "Summary and conclusions" completes the chapter.

Key words: bank competition, bank risk, GMM, Chinese banking.

Theory of bank competition

In much the same way as other industries, the types of competition in the banking sector can be classified in the following categories: perfect competition (also called pure competition), monopolistic competition, oligopoly, and monopoly. The perfect competitive environment in the banking sector has the following characteristics: (1) there are a large number of banks in the market; (2) banks offer homogeneous products regarding product costs and attributes; (3) the cost of entry to the market is very low. In a perfectly competitive environment, banks are price-takers rather than price-makers. The price of products offered by banks will be determined by supply and demand but banks will have no ability to influence supply and demand in the market.

Another type of competition is monopolistic competition. Under this competitive environment, there are lots of banks in the market. Unlike the situation in a perfectly competitive market, banks offer differentiated products to customers. The cost of entry to and exit from the banking market is low; however, it is higher than the corresponding cost in a perfectly competitive market. Banks have a degree of control over the price of the product offered. In other words, they are to some extent price-makers rather than price-takers.

Another type of competition is oligopoly. Under this competitive environment, there are a small number of banks in the market, all of which provide either homogeneous or heterogeneous products. Entry to or exit from the market is expensive. Banks operating in an oligopoly have the power to set the price in the market. Unlike monopolistic competition, the degree of price control by banks in an oligopoly is higher. An oligopoly differs from monopolistic competition and perfect competition by the interdependence exhibited by banks. As a result of the small number of banks in an oligopoly and each bank being of similar size, the action of every bank can affect market conditions. Thus, other banks will be aware of a single bank's action and respond appropriately in order to maintain its own competitive position in the market.

Finally, in a monopoly there is only one banking firm in the market. Banking under such an environment is not subject to competition, it is impossible for potential banks to enter the market, and banks have absolute control over the price charged for the services provided. They also have the ability to charge different prices to different markets. For example, they can charge lower prices in a very elastic market to increase the quantity of products sold and higher prices in a relatively inelastic market to maximize profit.

Structure–conduct–performance theory

The structure–conduct–performance (SCP) paradigm argues that market structure is a determinant of firm conduct, which in turn determines performance. Market structure can be measured by a number of factors such as the number of competitors in an industry, the heterogeneity of products, and the cost of entry and exit. Conduct refers to specific actions taken by firms such as price-taking, product differentiation, tacit collusion, and exploitation of market power. The performance of a firm can be reflected by a number of indicators such as productive efficiency, allocative efficiency, and profitability.

The range of options and constraints facing a firm are defined by the attributes of the industry within which it operates. In industries where competition is high, not only are there very few options available to firms but there are many constraints as well. Firms in these industries maximize social welfare and in the long run returns only cover the cost of capital. In short, industry structure determines firm conduct and long-run firm performance. On the other hand, firms operating in an environment where competition is low not only have a greater range of options but the number of constraints they face are limited. Firms can make use of whatever options are

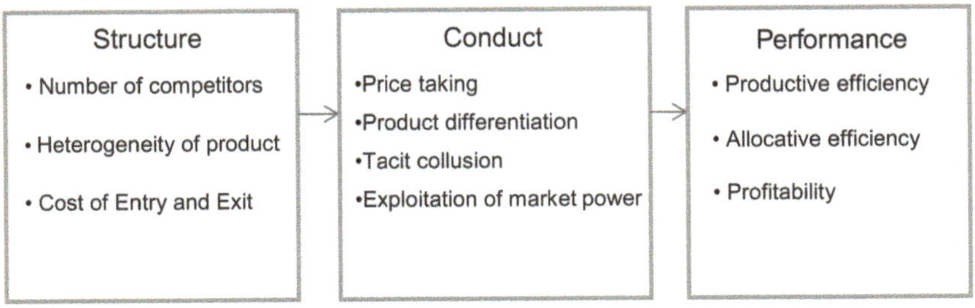

Figure 5.1 **The structure–conduct–performance model**

available to gain competitive advantage. For instance, firms in these industries can use market power to set prices that generate significant economic value. However, the sustainability of their advantage depends on barriers to entry – an attribute of industry structure. If there are no barriers to entry, the competitive advantage of firms in the industry will disappear when new competitors enter the market. Thus, firms should adopt competitive strategies to sustain their competitive advantage and superior performance. Therefore, industry structure has an important effect on firm conduct and firm performance even though firms in these industries sometimes have competitive advantage. The SCP model is summarized in Figure 5.1.

Lerner index

The Lerner index was developed in 1934 by American economist Abba Lerner. It is defined as the difference between price and marginal cost divided by price and can be specified as

$$LI_{it} = (P_{it} - MC_{it})/P_{it}$$

where P is the price of banking outputs; MC represents margin cost; and i and t represent a specific bank in a specific year. The value of the Lerner index ranges from a minimum of zero to a maximum of one. When $P = MC$, the Lerner index is zero, which indicates the firm has no pricing power. As the value of the Lerner index increases, the difference between price and marginal cost becomes larger, which indicates that banks have higher market power (Ariss, 2010). In other words, $LI = 0$ indicates that there is perfect competition while $LI = 1$ means the market is monopolistic.

Casu and Girardone (2009) argue that the Lerner index is a good measure of monopolistic power, and that the banking literature has adopted it as an effective and widely used indicator to measure competition. It represents the extent to which banks have the market power to set their own prices above marginal cost (Berger et al., 2009). A similar opinion is held by Demirguc-Kunt and Peria (2010) who suggest that computing direct measures of market power is an alternative way of examining competitive conditions in the banking industry, and that the Lerner index is frequently used in the banking sector. Lerner (1934) argues that market power is determined by demand elasticity, and that the Lerner index provides a means of measuring demand price elasticity (inverse relationship). Rojas (2011) suggests that the Lerner index is popular because it shows where a firm's market power lies along the perfect competition and monopoly continuum, and that it reflects the role demand elasticity plays in determining a firm's markup. Compared with the traditional concentration ratio, the Lerner index provides a more accurate measurement of bank market power; while the advantage the Lerner index has over the Panzar–Rosse H-statistic (which will be explained in the next subsection) lies in it not being a long-run equilibrium measure of competition but in the ease with which it can be calculated for each bank and for each year (Degryse et al., 2009).

There are also arguments pointing up the disadvantages of the Lerner index. Fernandez de Guevara et al. (2005) argue that there are several problems when estimating the Lerner index. First, the value of the Lerner index changes according to different revenues used in their study. It is frequently the case that only interest and costs are considered while other non-interest revenues and expenses are omitted. Considering traditional loan–deposit services as revenue ignores the banking activities of providing other services that have grown substantially during recent years. This will lead to an inaccurate result when it comes to calculating competitive conditions in the banking sector. Second, the cost of risk, which is very important in the profit and loss account of banks, is generally not considered at all. Ignoring the cost of risk can be attributed to issues like insufficient data and calculation difficulties. If the cost of risk is not included when estimating the cost function, the Lerner index will be interpreted incorrectly because margins are overestimated. Third, Bikker et al. (2007) argue that another weakness of the Lerner index is that the prices and costs required to calculate the index are not clearly identified by available bank balance sheet data, which leads to prices and costs being proxied for by many debatable factors.

Panzar–Rosse (1987) H-statistic

John C. Panzar and James N. Rosse developed an empirical test to discriminate between monopolistic, oligopolistic, monopolistically competitive, and perfectly competitive markets. They provided a concise indicator (the so-called H-statistic), which was based on the static properties of the reduced form revenue equation. The H-statistic can be interpreted as a continuous and increasing measure of the overall level of competition in a specific market. This method makes the assumption that different pricing strategies will be

Table 5.1 Discriminatory power of the H-statistic

Estimated value of H	Competitive environment	Market equilibrium
$H \leq 0$	Monopolistic market behaviour	$H = 0$: equilibrium
	Conjectural variation of short-run oligopoly	$H \neq 0$: disequilibrium
$0 \leq H < 1$	Monopolistic competition	
$H = 1$	Natural monopoly in a perfectly contestable market	
	Perfect competition	

employed as a reaction to change in input costs. In other words, market power is measured by the extent to which changes in factor prices (unit price of funds, capital, and labour) are reflected in revenue.

The H-statistic ranges from $-\infty$ to 1 (see Table 5.1). A negative H arises when the competitive structure is a monopoly, a perfectly colluding oligopoly, or a conjectural variation of a short-run oligopoly. In all cases an increase in input price will translate into higher marginal costs, a reduction of equilibrium output, and a subsequent fall in total revenue (Vesala, 1995). If H lies between 0 and 1, the market structure is one of monopolistic competition. Under monopolistic competition, potential entry leads to equilibrium in a contestable market and revenue increases less than proportionally to changes in input prices, because the demand for banking products facing individual banks is inelastic (Triole, 1987). Under perfect competition, the H-statistic equals 1. In this particular situation, a proportional increase in factor input prices raises both marginal and average costs and induces an equiproportional change in revenues without distorting the optimal output of any firm. The H-statistic is also equal to 1 if there is a contestable market. Baumol et al. (1982), who put forward the contestability theory, argue that under very restrictive circumstances, such as free entry and exit to the market and higher price elasticity of demand for industrial output, competition in highly concentrated markets still exists. Larger firms in the market need to adopt competitive approaches to pricing their outputs as a result of these factors.

As use of the H-statistic is deemed a static approach, the test needs to be undertaken on observations that are in long-run equilibrium. In other words, the dependent variable in an equilibrium test will be replaced by a profitability measure, such as return on assets (ROA) or return on equity (ROE), rather than revenue. In equilibrium the resulting H-statistic will be significantly equal to 0. However, a significant and negative H-statistic indicates that the test is not in long-run equilibrium.

The advantages of using the Panzar–Rosse H-statistic to measure competition are: (1) it works well with firm-specific data on revenue and factor prices; (2) it does not require information about equilibrium output prices and quantities for the firm and/or industry; (3) it can calculate the concise competitive condition if the sample size is small (Matthews et al., 2007); (4) it can include bank-specific factors in the production function (Mensi, 2010); (5) it has the advantage of simplicity and transparency without losing efficiency (Negrin et al., 2006). As a result of the H-statistic being developed as a static approach, it cannot predict an H-value, one of its weaknesses. In addition, as a result of the test requiring overall market equilibrium the test cannot be fulfilled because of market entry and exit, which leads to further limits on the interpretation of such analysis.

Methodology behind estimating bank competition

Estimation of bank competition (Panzar–Rosse H-statistic)

The following reduced form revenue equation (Eq. 5.1) is selected in empirical analysis to derive the Panzar–Rosse H-statistic:

$$\begin{aligned}\text{Ln}\, TR_{it} = {} & \alpha + \beta_1 \text{Ln}\, P_{1,it} + \beta_2 \text{Ln}\, P_{2,it} + \beta_3 \text{Ln}\, P_{3,it} \\ & + \gamma_1 \text{Ln}\, QUAST_{it} + \gamma_2 \text{Ln}\, LOANAST_{it} \\ & + \gamma_3 \text{Ln}\, OIAST_{it} + \varepsilon_{it} \qquad (5.1)\end{aligned}$$

for $t = 1, \ldots, T$, where T is the number of periods observed; and for $i = 1, \ldots, I$, where I is the total number of banks. Subscripts i and t refer to bank i at time t. The dependent variable TR is total revenue over total assets. The reason total revenue is used instead of interest revenue is that non-interest income from fee-based products and off-balance-sheet activities has increased dramatically in recent years. As argued by De Bandt and Davis (2000), the distinction between interest and non-interest income in a more competitive environment becomes less relevant and more banks compete on both fronts. Finally, the ratio of total revenue to total assets rather than total revenue is considered the dependent variable that accounts for size difference.

Consistent with the intermediation approach,[1] it is assumed that banks use three inputs: deposits, labour, and capital. Ln P_1 is the average cost of funds (interest expenses/total funds), Ln P_2 is the average cost of labour (personnel expenses/total assets), and Ln P_3 is the average cost of capital (other operating expenses/fixed assets).

The right-hand side of the equation includes a set of bank-specific variables that reflect the differences in capitalization (*QUAST*), liquidity (*LOANAST*), and product mix (*OIAST*) necessary for bank heterogeneity. These variables are the ratio of equity to total assets, the ratio of loans to total assets, and the ratio of other income to total assets.

The ratio of other income to total assets (*OIAST*) is included as an explanatory variable to account for the influence the generation of other income has on the model's underlying marginal revenue and cost functions. The coefficient of capitalization is expected to be negative because lower capital ratios lead to higher bank revenue (Molyneux et al., 1994). However, the higher the capital ratio the more risky the loan portfolio and the higher the bank revenue. This positive effect is supported by Coccorese (2004).

The ratio of loans to total assets is used to control for bank liquidity. The coefficient is expected to be positive because higher proportions of loans in a bank's total assets normally lead to higher bank revenue.

The ratio of other income to total assets is used to control for the differences in business mix. A positive coefficient is expected because a higher volume of non-interest income contributes to greater bank revenue.

An important feature of the Panzar–Rosse H-statistic is that it can only be carried out on data representing a market in long-run equilibrium. This suggests that competitive capital markets equalize the risk-adjusted rate of return across banks such that rates of return in equilibrium are uncorrelated with input prices (Molyneux et al., 1994). Moreover, a long-run equilibrium test can only be carried out using the H-statistic, when it measures the sum of elasticity of return on assets with respect to input prices as shown in Eq. 5.2.

The resulting H-statistic is expected to be significantly equal to 0 in equilibrium and significantly negative in the case of disequilibrium (Shaffer, 1982; Molyneux et al., 1994; Claessens and Laeven, 2004):

$$\begin{aligned} \text{Ln } ROA_{it} &= \alpha + \beta_1 \text{ Ln } P_{1,it} + \beta_2 \text{ Ln } P_{2,it} + \beta_3 \text{ Ln } P_{3,it} \\ &\quad + \gamma_1 \text{ Ln } QUAST_{it} + \gamma_2 \text{ Ln } LOANAST_{it} \\ &\quad + \gamma_3 \text{ Ln } OIAST_{it} + \varepsilon_{it} \end{aligned} \tag{5.2}$$

The small negative values of ROA incurred by some banks in a specific year are taken into account in Eq. 5.2 by using $\text{Ln}(1 + ROA)$ as the dependent variable. The equilibrium statistics that result from Eq. 5.2 can be tested using an F-test.

Measurement of bank competition (Lerner index)

Price is estimated by taking the average price of bank production (proxied for by total assets) as the ratio of total revenue to total assets following Fernandez de Guevara et al. (2005) and Carbo-Valverde et al. (2009). Marginal cost is estimated on the basis of a translog cost function with one output (total assets) and three input prices (price of labour, price of capital, and price of funds). Symmetry and linear homogeneity restrictions on input prices are imposed. The cost function is specified as:

$$\begin{aligned} \text{Ln } TC &= \alpha_0 + \alpha_1 \text{ Ln } Y + \frac{1}{2}\alpha_2(\text{Ln } Y)^2 + \sum_{j=1}^{3} \beta_j \text{ Ln } W_j \\ &\quad + \sum_{j=1}^{3}\sum_{k=1}^{3} \beta_{jk} \text{ Ln } W_j \text{ Ln } W_k \sum_{j=1}^{3} \gamma_j \text{ Ln } Y \text{ Ln } W_j + \varepsilon \end{aligned} \tag{5.3}$$

where TC denotes total cost; Y represents total assets; W_1 is the price of funds (ratio of interest expenses to total funding); W_2 indicates the price of capital (ratio of other non-interest expenses to fixed assets); and W_3 stands for the price of labour (ratio of personnel expenses to total assets). The indices for each bank and each time have been dropped from the presentation for the sake of simplicity. The estimated coefficients of the cost function can now be used to compute marginal cost (MC):

$$MC = \frac{TC}{Y}\left(\alpha_1 + \alpha_2 \text{ Ln } Y + \sum_{j=1}^{3} \gamma_j \text{ Ln } W_j\right) \tag{5.4}$$

Once marginal cost is estimated and the price of output computed, we can calculate the Lerner index for each bank and obtain a direct measure of bank competition.

Modelling the impact competition has on risk/stability

Following Liu and Wilson (2013), an estimable model is outlined to capture the impact competition has on risk in the Chinese banking industry while controlling for the range of bank-specific and macroeconomic covariates that have been widely used to examine the drivers of bank stability. The model can be expressed as:

$$\begin{aligned}\delta_{it} = \beta_0 + \lambda\delta_{i,t-1} + \beta_1\, competition_{it} + \beta_2\, competition_{it}^2 \\ + \beta_3 X_{it} + \beta_4 M_t + \mu_i + \nu_{it}\end{aligned} \tag{5.5}$$

where subscripts i and t denote bank i at year t; δ_{it} is the bank stability/risk measure, which are the ratio of loan loss provision over total loans (LLPTL), the Z-score, and the stability inefficiency; $\delta_{i,t-1}$ is the one-period lag bank stability measure; $competition_{it}$ is the bank competition measure, which is either the Panzar–Rosse H-statistic, the Lerner index, or the three-bank concentration ratio; $competition_{it}^2$ is the quadratic term of bank competition addressing the non-linear relationship between competition and risk found by Martinez-Miera and Repullo (2010); X_{it} is a vector of exogenous bank-specific variables; M_{it} is a vector of macroeconomic variables; μ_{it} is a fixed effect; and ν_{it} is random disturbance.

The one-step General Method of Moments (GMM) estimator of Arellano and Bover (1995) and Blundell and Bond (1998) is used to estimate the equation. Compared with the two-step GMM system estimator employed by Liu and Wilson (2013), the one-step GMM estimator is preferred because it outperforms the two-step estimator in producing both a smaller bias and estimates that have a smaller standard deviation (Judson and Owen, 1999). The lagged dependent variable (risk/stability measure) is included in the regression. Moreover, second and higher order lags and differences of the dependent variable are used to solve the endogeneity problem. The results provide the necessary information for overidentifying restrictions to be tested by the Sargan test as well as for first and second-order autocorrelation of the error term.

It was considered best to use lagged values for the covariates in the equation to address the endogeneity issues. Overhead cost – an indicator of bank efficiency and measured by the ratio of overhead cost over total assets – is expected to be positively related to bank risk. Boyd et al. (2006) and Agoraki et al. (2009) argue that less efficient banks (higher overhead cost) are likely to take on higher risk to generate return to improve performance.

Liquidity (*LTA*), which is measured by the ratio between loans and assets, is supposed to be negatively related to bank risk because when this ratio is high banks experience greater loan exposure and when the volume of funds available is low the ability of banks to deal with daily withdrawals by customers is reduced, which further increases the possibility of bankruptcy and higher bank risk.

Bank size (Ln *TA*), which is measured by the natural logarithm of total assets, is expected to be negatively related to bank risk. Berger (1995) argues that higher stability (lower risks) can be achieved by larger banks because of economies of scale and market power. However, the higher returns generated by higher risk projects can give rise to managers of larger banks taking on higher risk. This is exacerbated because large institutions considered too big to fail by the government are fully aware that they will get bailed out if they get into trouble (Stern and Feldman, 2004; Herring and Carmassi, 2010; Demirguc-Kunt and Huizinga, 2010). Thus, the relationship between bank size and risk is unclear.

Diversification (*NTA*), which is measured by the ratio between non-interest income and gross revenue, is expected to be negatively related to bank risk. Stiroh (2010) argues that risk can be reduced as a result of improved efficiency via economies of scale and scope. However, Beck et al. (2009), Demirguc-Kunt and Huizinga (2010), and Liu and Wilson (2013) show that the performance of banks that engage in more diversified activities is less stable than banks engaging in less diversified business. Thus, there is no *a priori* expectation of the impact diversification has on bank risk in China.

Inflation and GDP growth (GDPG) are the two macroeconomic variables used in this study to look at the effect the macroeconomic environment has on bank risk in China. The annual inflation rate is expected to be negatively related to bank risk. Lown and Morgan (2006) and Buch et al. (2010) argue that the financial system and the economy are adversely affected by inflation. Moreover, decision-making is distorted, information asymmetry is exacerbated, and price volatility becomes the norm when inflation is high. The GDP growth rate is expected to be positively related to bank risk. Much of the literature has found that during economic booms financial institutions are more likely to lend excessively, while their lending behaviour will be more cautious during economic downturns (Berger and Udell, 2004; Dell'Ariccia and Marquez, 2006).

Literature review

Investigation of the competitive condition in the Chinese banking sector

There are very few studies examining the competitive condition of the Chinese banking sector. The competitive condition of Chinese banking between 1996 and 2000 was evaluated by Yuan (2006), who used a Panzar–Rosse model. The results indicated that the banking sector in China was closer to perfect competition than any other. Using a Panzar–Rosse model, the competitive condition of 76 Chinese banks between 1997 and 2007 was investigated by Fu (2009). The findings suggested the Chinese banking sector was in a state of monopolistic competition. Furthermore, she argued that the core market for bank lending underwent higher competition, while the competitive condition of the off-balance-sheet market was relatively lower. Using the same method, Masood and Sergi (2011) examined the competitive condition of 16 Chinese banks between 2004 and 2007. The findings showed the Chinese banking sector to be in a state of monopolistic competition. In a more recent study, Park (2013) used the Panzar–Rosse H-statistic to measure the competitive condition of 15 Chinese commercial banks between 1992 and 2008. The results indicated the competitive condition of the Chinese banking sector was closer to oligopoly than any other. Using a large sample of banks operating in China during 1996–2008, Xu et al. (2013) investigated the competitive condition of the Chinese banking industry. The findings suggested that the bank lending markets in China had been more competitive. Finally, using four different risk indicators – the ratio of loan loss provision over total loans, the volatility of ROA, the volatility of ROE and the Z-score – Tan and Floros (2014) used the Lerner index as the competition indicator to investigate the interrelationship between risk and competition for a sample of Chinese commercial banks over the period 2003–09. Empirical findings suggested that competition had no significant impact on the risk-taking behaviour of Chinese commercial banks.

The impact competition has on the risk-taking behaviour of Chinese banks

Several rounds of banking reforms in China have had the objective of improving the competitive condition of the Chinese banking sector. The Asian financial crisis of 2007 prompted the government to look at the risk-taking behaviour of banks much more critically. The empirical literature argues that competition has a significant impact on the risk-taking behaviour of banks, and that the effect is supported by two hypotheses: the competition–stability hypothesis and the competition–fragility hypothesis.

Competition–stability hypothesis

The competition–stability hypothesis states that in a competitive environment banks tend to experience lower risk and, hence, the banking sector is more stable (Boyd and De Nicolo, 2005).

Boyd and De Nicolo (2005) argue that the cost of borrowing for consumers in a more concentrated loan market is higher, while their success in servicing their investment is lower. This is believed to lead to a higher probability of loan default. Thus, they argue that the impact bank competition has on risk is significant and negative. Mishkin (1999) supports this hypothesis. He argues that there are fewer banks in a more concentrated banking market and, as a result of the government being scared of bank failure (the too-big-to-fail issue), subsidies and other favours are granted to these banks, which gives rise to bank managers being less careful when it comes to credit checking, monitoring, and allocation. Such carelessness inexorably leads to an increase in risk-taking behaviour and a less stable banking environment.

Beck (2008) points out that there are fewer banks in a more concentrated banking market where competition is lower, and that they are larger, more complicated, and difficult to manage. Such banks are hard to monitor and may well be prone to higher risk and lower stability.

Competition–fragility hypothesis

The competition–fragility hypothesis accords with the charter value[2] view modelled by Marcus (1984), Chan et al. (1986), and Keeley (1990), which argues that higher competition in a banking sector gives rise to bank managers taking higher risks. According to the conventional risk–return hypothesis, higher risk always results in higher profitability, but the higher risk-taking behaviour of banks leads to greater fragility in the banking sector. Boot and Greenbaum (1993) and Allen and Gale (2000, 2004) argue that the informational rent banks get from their borrowers is reduced in a more competitive environment, which reduces their incentive to monitor borrowers. In this sense the banking sector becomes less stable. On the other hand, better profit will be achieved and higher capital levels held by banks in a less competitive environment, which reduces the incentive to undertake higher risk. This leads to higher financial stability. Moreover, in a more competitive environment the probability of a bank run will increase because of higher deposit rates, and margins will be lower. This leads to bank managers tending to take excessive risks, which results in greater fragility in the banking sector (Carletti, 2005).

The negative impact competition has on stability can also be explained from the perspective of interbank payment systems. Banks in a more competitive banking market are price-takers and those with high liquidity levels have no incentive to help counterparts experiencing liquidity problems. The failure of such banks will have a negative impact on the whole banking sector, which leads to greater fragility (Allen and Gale, 2000). However, Saez and Shi (2004) argue that banks experiencing temporary liquidity shortages are helped by some other banks.

Apart from these two hypotheses, recent research conducted by Martinez-Miera and Repullo (2010) argues that neither competition–stability nor competition–fragility hold. They argue that the relationship between competition and risk is non-linear. They suggest that the impact competition has on risk can result in one of two effects: the risk-shifting effect and the margin effect. The risk-shifting effect argues that higher competition reduces the probability of default of borrowers, which leads to a reduction in bank risk. The margin effect argues that interest payments from performing loans will be lower when competition is stronger, the reduction in interest payments increases bank risk. They further indicate that the relationship between competition and bank stability is U shaped. In other words, the risk-shifting effect dominates in markets that are more concentrated and increased competition decreases the risk-taking behaviour of banks, while the margin effect dominates in markets where there is more competition and greater competition leads to higher risk.

Empirical results

Competitive condition of Chinese banking

Figure 5.2 shows the competitive condition of Chinese banking between 2003 and 2011. Using the Lerner index (Figure 5.2a) the author found that city commercial banks (CCBs) experienced lower competition between 2004 and 2009. The reason for this was that, unlike state-owned commercial banks (SOCBs) and joint stock commercial banks (JSCBs), most CCBs were not listed on any stock exchange, their funds were mainly from local governments, and they had no incentive to compete to get funds from the public. JSCBs experienced the highest competition over the examined period. The reason for this was that, unlike SOCBs, which are fully supported by the Chinese government, JSCBs depended on contributions from shareholders. The incentive to attract more shareholders maximizes competition. When the competitive condition of the Chinese banking sector is looked at by year, which is measured by the three-bank concentration ratio (Figure 5.2b), it can be seen that the assets held by the three largest SOCBs continued to increase until 2009, when the figure dropped dramatically before climbing up to the highest point in 2010. Figure 5.2b shows that competition in the Chinese banking sector was still low and that the dramatic decline in concentration in 2009 could be explained by the 2008 Olympic Games in China acted as a catalyst for more financial institutions from around the world to open offices in China. The peak in the concentration ratio in 2010 can be partly explained by the fact that Chinese state-owned banks expanded their business operation overseas and that SOCBs still dominated the Chinese banking industry.

Using the Panzar–Rosse H-statistic (Figure 5.2c) the author estimates the competitive condition of the Chinese banking

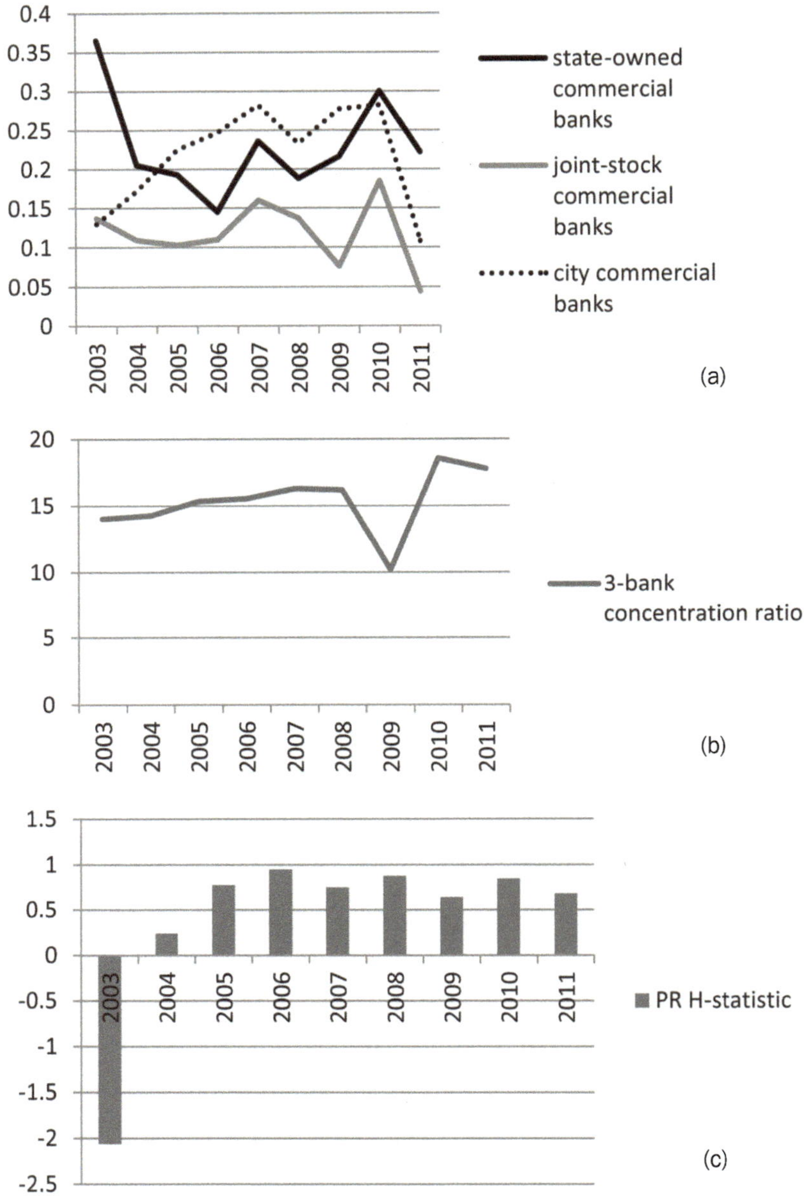

Figure 5.2 **Competitive condition of Chinese banking sector over the period 2003–11**

Competition measured by (a) Lerner index, (b) three-bank concentration ratio, and (c) Panzar–Rosse H statistic.

sector between 2003 and 2011. The figure shows the Panzar–Rosse H-statistic in 2003 to be −2.06, the lowest figure over the examined period. It suggests that competition in the Chinese banking sector was lowest in that year.

This finding indicates that the Chinese banking sector at that time was operating under monopolistic conditions. This can be explained by the Chinese government initiating in 2003 a pilot overhaul programme, which injected capital into SOCBs. The program not only improved capital levels and reduced the volume of non-performing loans in SOCBs, it decreased the competitive condition among Chinese banks as well. Figure 5.2c further shows that the Chinese banking sector experienced stronger competition in 2005, when the Panzar–Rosse H-statistic was 0.78, which can mainly be attributed to the initial public offering of one SOCB, the China Construction Bank, which was successfully listed on the Hong Kong Stock Exchange in 2005; as a consequence the competitive condition among state-owned commercial banks improved substantially.

The competitive condition of the Chinese banking sector further increased in 2006 with a Panzar–Rosse H-statistic of 0.95. This can be explained by another two SOCBs getting listed on stock exchanges in 2006: the Industrial and Commercial Bank of China was listed on both the Shanghai and Hong Kong stock exchanges, while the Bank of China was successfully listed on the Hong Kong Stock Exchange.

The slightly lower competition in 2005 as opposed to 2006 can be attributed to the non-performing loans of SOCBs being written off by four asset management companies. The improvement in the competitive condition of the Chinese banking sector in 2007 can be attributed to it being fully open to foreign competition. In other words, by the end of 2006 no restrictions were imposed on foreign bank services in China and foreign banks were treated exactly the same as domestic banks.

Table 5.2 Panzar–Rosse H-statistic over the period 2003–11

Year/variables	Intercept	P1	P2	P3	QUAST	LOANAST	OIAST	R2	H	C
					2003–11					
Coefficient (t-statistic)	−6.02 (−11)[c]	0.33 (2.2)[b]	0.4 (2.55)[b]	0.02 (0.3)	0.21 (4.3)[c]	0.22 (1.85)[a]	0.04 (1.62)	0.2620	0.6	Monopolistic competition
					2003					
Coefficient (t-statistic)	0.16 (0.01)	3.91 (0.79)	-1.93 (−0.96)	-4.04 (−1.2)	1.04 (1.39)	0.31 (−0.08)	0.97 (1.67)	0.9391	— 2.06	Monopoly
					2004					
Coefficient (t-statistic)	−5.75 (−2.40)	-0.14 (−0.4)	0.57 (1.52)	-0.18 (−0.4)	0.06 (0.43)	0.35 (0.54)	0.05 (0.83)	0.6274	0.24	Monopolistic competition
					2005					
Coefficient (t-statistic)	−5.91 (−3.93)[b]	0.49 (0.82)	0.69 (2.02)	-0.23 (−0.5)	0.06 (0.38)	0.17 (0.92)	0.05 (0.87)	0.88	0.78	Monopolistic competition
					2006					
Coefficient (t-statistic)	-6.54 (−6.16)	-0.05 (−0.2)	0.48 (1.11)	-0.06 (−0.3)	0.2 (2.18)[b]	0.51 (2.54)[b]	-0.05 (−1.10)	0.5347	0.95	Monopolistic competition

2007										
Coefficient (T-statistic)	−5.82 (−7.6)[c]	0.08 (0.34)	−0.12 (−0.70)	0.03 (0.28)	0.2 (3.42)[c]	0.47 (2.01)[a]	0.06 (1.62)	0.5377	0.75	Monopoly
2008										
Coefficient (T-statistic)	−5.54 (−10.8)[b]	−0.34 (−1.6)	0.41 (2.44)[b]	0.13 (1.57)	0.15 (2.29)[b]	0.34 (3.26)[c]	0.007 (0.23)	0.538	0.88	Monopolistic competition
2009										
Coefficient (t-statistic)	−6.9 (−9.2)[c]	0.21 (0.51)	0.32 (1.49)	0.11 (1.19)	0.25 (2.9)[c]	0.43 (2.61)[b]	0.38 (1.30)	0.4574	0.64	Monopolistic competition
2010										
Coefficient (t-statistic)	−5.35 (−8.8)[c]	0.4 (0.78)	0.55 (1.22)	0.28 (0.35)	0.18 (2.55)[c]	0.48 (3.53)[c]	0.05 (1.58)	0.6338	0.85	Monopolistic competition
2011										
Coefficient (t-statistic)	-6.16 (−2.88)	0.38 (0.65)	0.58 (1.28)	0.22 (0.28)	0.23 (2.56)[b]	0.53 (2.58)[c]	0.06 (1.65)	0.5386	0.68	Monopolistic competition

[a], 10 per cent level of significance; [b], 5 per cent level of significance; [c], 1 per cent level of significance

The Panzar–Rosse H-statistic for the Chinese banking sector was 0.88 in 2008, which likely reflected the fact that the Olympic Games not only stimulated foreign investment in China but increased the number of foreign financial institutions in China, which in turn substantially improved the competitive condition of the banking industry. A similar situation happened in 2010 when the last SOCB, the Agricultural Bank of China, was successfully listed on the Shanghai and Hong Kong stock exchanges in July, becoming the largest initial public offering ever in banking history. In August of the same year the JSCB China Everbright Bank was listed on the Shanghai Stock Exchange. These two listings increased the competitive condition of the Chinese banking sector.

The impact competition has on the risk-taking behaviour of Chinese banks

Table 5.3 shows how bank risk is affected when competition is measured by the Lerner index. The findings suggest that the coefficients of loan loss provision over total loans and Z-scores have positive and negative signs, respectively and both are statistically significant, which indicates that Chinese bank risk is relatively higher under more competitive conditions. This result indicates that the Chinese banking sector accords with the competition–fragility hypothesis. However, the findings further show that the quadratic term of competition is significant when risk is measured by the Z-score, which indicates the impact competition has on bank risk (Z-score) is non-linear. In other words, the findings confirm that greater competition leads to a higher volume of loan loss provision of Chinese commercial banks. The ratio of loan loss provision over total loans focusses on the risk that comes from traditional loan–deposit services. Despite several rounds of banking reforms increasing the ability of banks to risk-manage, the increased competition results in bank managers failing to monitor risk, which leads to an increase in bank risk. This is clearly reflected in the volume of loan loss provisions.

As far as bank-specific variables are concerned, it can be seen that bank size is significant for all risk indicators. Significant and negative signs are the norm when risk is measured by the ratio of loan loss provision over total loans and stability inefficiency, while a positive sign is shown when the Z-score is used as the risk indicator. The results suggest that bank size is significantly and negatively related to bank risk. In other words, larger Chinese banks normally have lower risk regarding the ratio between loan loss provision and total loans. Chinese banks with greater assets such as SOCBs can get the number of non-performing loans reduced either by capital injections from the government or by getting their non-performing loans written off by the four asset management companies set up by the government for the very purpose. Furthermore, compared with JSCBs and CCBs, large SOCBs have more experience and greater ability when it comes to risk management, which leads to a reduction in loan loss provisions. On the other hand, as far as stability inefficiency and the Z-score are concerned, the results indicate that larger Chinese banks are not only better able to meet their financial obligations, they are more stable. This can be explained by large SOCBs being fully supported by the government. Since they are considered too big to fail, the government will help them out whenever there is an insolvency issue.

The results indicate that overhead cost is significantly and positively related to risk when risk is measured by the ratio of loan loss provision over total loans. Overhead cost shows the ability of bank managers to control costs. The findings suggest that Chinese banks with higher levels of overhead costs normally experience higher risk in terms of loan loss

Table 5.3 Empirical results (Lerner index as competition indicator)

	Risk (ratio of loan loss provision over total loans)		Risk (Z-score)		Risk (stability inefficiency)	
	Coefficient	T-statistic	Coefficient	T-statistic	Coefficient	T-statistic
Lag of dependent variable	0.23[c]	4.68	–0.029	–0.18	–0.74[c]	–27.91
Competition	–0.02[b]	–2.02	6,192.9[c]	2.9	0.07	0.42
Competition^2	0.005	0.15	–12,453[c]	-2.73	0.036	0.11
Bank-specific variables						
Bank size	–0.001[c]	–5.11	511.82[c]	8.18	–0.01[b]	–2.21
Bank liquidity	0.00001	0.39	3.005	0.33	–0.00002	–0.04
Non-traditional activity	–8.76e–06	-0.30	–1.72	-0.21	0.001[a]	1.81
Overhead cost	0.63[c]	5.97	253,266[c]	9.10	–2.53	–1.26

Macroeconomics						
GDP growth rate	−0.0004[c]	−2.73	27	0.71	−0.016[c]	−6.02
Annual inflation rate	0.0007[c]	5.72	65.85[b]	2.04	−0.006[b]	−2.34
F test	123.97[c]		102.13[c]		471.49[c]	
Sargan test	48.87		76.21		268.20	
AR(1)	$Z = -4.54$	$P = 0.000$	$Z = -0.32$	$P = 0.747$	$Z = -1.48$	$P = 0.138$
AR(2)	$Z = 0.63$	$P = 0.523$	$Z = -0.46$	$P = 0.645$	$Z = -0.56$	$P = 0.576$
No. of observations	155		128		174	

[a], 10 per cent level of significance; [b], 5 per cent level of significance; [c], 1 per cent level of significance.
Competition^2 is the square term of competition and captures the non-linear impact of competition on the risk-taking behaviour of banks.

provision. As reported in Table 4.4, SOCBs and CCBs have similar overhead costs both of which are higher than JSCBs. In other words, the results indicate that SOCBs and CCBs have a larger volume of loan loss provisions. This finding can be explained by the following. The managers in SOCBs have less incentive to monitor and manage bank risk because of the too-big-to-fail consideration. As a result of CCBs mainly serving local small-sized enterprises, the capital levels of which are much lower than large and medium-sized enterprises, the lower capital levels of these enterprises further increase the probability of loan default and increase the levels of loan loss provisions of CCBs. On the other hand, it can be seen that banks with overhead costs have lower risk and greater stability (when risk is measured by the Z-score). This finding can be explained by the fact that SOCBs and CCBs, which have higher overhead costs than JSCBs, are supported by central government and local city government, respectively.

As far as macroeconomic variables are concerned, the results show that the GDP growth rate has significant and negative signs when risk is measured by the ratio of loan loss provision over total loans and stability inefficiency. This indicates that the volume of loan loss provision of Chinese banks during booms is relatively lower and that Chinese banks are more stable. The higher GDP growth in China during recent years can mainly be attributed to a couple of factors. (1) Large government-funded projects like the high-speed train system. The government invested huge amounts of money in recent years to get this built. The high-speed train systems linking Beijing to Tianjin and Beijing to Shanghai are particularly important. Large government- funded projects like this stimulate the development of different industries in the economic sector and have the knock-on effect of further reducing the default rate and the volume of loan loss provision. (2) The 2008 Olympic Games in China was the catalyst for foreign investors to launch projects in China and, more importantly, for financial institutions to open offices in China. This brought more experience and knowledge to Chinese financial institutions regarding risk management and, as a result, the volume of loan loss provision was reduced and the stability of the whole banking sector enhanced.

As far as the impact inflation has on the risk-taking behaviour of Chinese banks, the results indicate that higher inflation rates lead to a higher volume of loan loss provision, as reflected by the significant and positive signs of this variable. The reason for this is that the amount of currency circulating in the market is greater than the value of the actual goods and services provided when inflation is higher. Adjustment of the reserve ratio is one of the measurements taken by the Chinese government to address this. Raising the reserve ratio reduces the money supply and the resulting increase in the interest rate raises the borrowing cost for the firms, which is supposed to lead to a decrease in firm profitabiltiy and further an increase in the probability of locan default. This variable has significant and positive signs when risk is measured by the Z-score and significant and negative signs when risk is measured by stability inefficiency, which indicates that higher inflation contributes to stability in the Chinese banking sector. As pointed out in Chapter 4, this can be explained by Chinese banks being able to anticipate the inflation rate and to adjust their own interest rates accordingly. This leads to a higher increase in bank revenue over costs and, therefore, bank profitability will increase at times of higher inflation. The higher profitability of Chinese banks promotes the stability of Chinese banks and improves their ability to meet financial obligations when they become due. Thus, higher inflation leads to a higher Z-score and lower stability inefficiency.

The impact competition has on the risk-taking behaviour of Chinese banks when competition is measured by the Panzar–

Table 5.4 Empirical results (Panzar–Rosse H-statistic as competition indicator)

	Risk (ratio of loan loss provision over total loans)		Risk (Z-score)		Risk (stability inefficiency)	
	Coefficient	**T-statistic**	**Coefficient**	**T-statistic**	**Coefficient**	**T-statistic**
Lag of dependent variable	0.22[c]	4.92	0.03	0.17	–0.26[c]	–7.83
Competition	–0.004[c]	–4.82	–78.2	–0.54	1.01[c]	13.52
Competition^2	0.003	1.25	–252.36[c]	–2.47	–0.26[c]	–3.19
Bank-specific variables						
Bank size	–0.001[c]	–3.25	311.19[c]	6.86	–0.03[c]	–8.05
Bank liquidity	0.0001	1.38	23.74[c]	3.01	–0.002[c]	–4.52
Non-traditional activity	0.00005[a]	1.76	12.12[b]	2.13	–0.001[c]	–2.86
Overhead cost	0.44[c]	4.43	187,313.2[c]	9.44	–6.76[c]	–5.31

Macroeconomics						
GDP growth rate	−0.001[c]	-3.3	15.8	0.59	0.05[c]	17.55
Annual inflation rate	0.0008[c]	5.31	15.8	0.59	0.03[c]	10.00
F test	159.17[c]		166.46[c]		1,024.38[c]	
Sargan test	89.10[c]		83.61[c]		611.30[c]	
AR(1)	$Z = -8.68$	$P = 0.000$	$Z = -3.06$	$P = 0.002$	$Z = -4.23$	$P = 0.000$
AR(2)	$Z = 0.39$	$P = 0.693$	$Z = 0.24$	$P = 0.810$	$Z = 0.83$	$P = 0.405$
No. of observations	325		256		402	

[a], 10 per cent level of significance; [b], 5 per cent level of significance; [c], 1 per cent level of significance.
$Competition^2$ is the square term of competition and captures the non-linear impact of competition on the risk-taking behaviour of banks.

Table 5.5 Empirical results (three bank concentration ratio as competition indicator)

	Risk (ratio of loan loss provision over total loans)		Risk (Z-score)		Risk (stability inefficiency)	
	Coefficient	**T-statistic**	**Coefficient**	**T-statistic**	**Coefficient**	**T-statistic**
Lag of dependent variable	0.064	1.35	0.03	0.17	–0.71[c]	–140.78
Competition	–0.018[b]	–2.05	–5144[c]	–2.76	–2.57[c]	–56.73
Competition2	0.0007	1.22	195.82[c]	2.86	0.098[c]	58.73
Bank-specific variables						
Bank size	–0.0008[c]	-3.37	513.9[c]	9.62	–0.0004	–0.40
Bank liquidity	0.00003	1.00	26.91[c]	3.17	0.0001	0.90
Non-traditional activity	–0.00002	–0.85	–8.66	–1.20	0.0001	0.98
Overhead cost	0.462[c]	4.78	1,674[c]	7.29	–0.124	–0.40

Macroeconomics						
GDP growth rate	-0.0008^{c}	−3.89	−52.9	−1.09	-0.045^{c}	−62.19
Annual inflation rate	0.0002^{c}	2.88	−58.09	−0.65	-0.006^{c}	−3.95
F test	120.24^{c}		102.84^{c}		$5.09e+06^{c}$	
Sargan test	38.08		62.98		637.82	
AR(1) (p-value)	$Z = -8.03$	$P = 0.000$	$Z = -3.34$	$P = 0.001$	$Z = -0.96$	$P = 0.337$
AR(2) (p-value)	$Z = 0.75$	$P = 0.453$	$Z = -00.89$	$P = 0.375$	$Z = 0.94$	$P = 0.349$
No. of observations	243		213		274	

[a], 10 per cent level of significance; [b], 5 per cent level of significance; [c], 1 per cent level of significance.
Competition^2 is the square term of competition and captures the non-linear impact of competition on the risk-taking behaviour of banks.

Rosse H-statistic and the three-bank concentration ratio (Tables 5.4 and 5.5, respectively), especially when compared with Table 5.3, proffers the following empirical findings: (1) larger Chinese banks normally have lower risk when measured by the ratio of loan loss provision over total loans; (2) larger Chinese banks normally have lower risk and higher stability when measured by the Z-score and stability inefficiency; (3) Chinese banks with higher overhead costs normally have higher risk in terms of loan loss provisions; (4) Chinese banks with higher levels of overhead costs normally have lower risk and more stability in terms of the Z-score and stability inefficiency; (5) during booms (higher GDP growth rate) the risk faced by the Chinese banking sector is lower (lower volume of loan loss provisions); (6) higher inflation leads to higher risk in terms of the volume of loan loss provision.

Comparison of the specific risk indicators in these three tables proffers the following findings: (1) when risk is measured by the ratio of loan loss provision over total loans, the results suggest that higher competition leads to higher Chinese bank risk; (2) larger Chinese banks normally have lower risk; (3) Chinese banks with higher levels of overhead costs normally have higher risk; (4) a higher GDP growth rate reduces Chinese bank risk; (4) Chinese banks have higher risk when inflation is higher. On the other hand, when risk is measured by the Z-score, the results suggest that larger Chinese banks with higher volumes of overhead costs are more stable.

Summary and conclusion

Banking reforms in China have brought about different ownerships of financial institutions, the purpose of which was to increase the competitive condition among different groups of banks and, in so doing, contribute to improving the performance of Chinese banks. The financial crisis of 2007 prompted the Chinese government and the banking regulatory authority to look at the risk-taking behaviour of Chinese banks. The empirical literature argues that higher competition likely gives rise to bank managers taking higher risks, which negatively influences the stability of the banking sector and the Chinese economy as a whole.

This chapter begins by presenting the theory of bank competition. This is followed by an explanation of the methodologies used to measure the competitive condition of Chinese banking sector. The econometric method used to investigate the impact bank competition has on bank risk is then presented. The chapter also reviews empirical research into the competitive condition of the Chinese banking sector. Two arguments are used to measure the impact bank competition has on bank risk: the competition–stability hypothesis and the competition–fragility hypothesis. This chapter measures the competitive condition using three different indicators: the Lerner index, the Panzar–Rosse H-statistic, and the three-bank concentration ratio. The competitive condition of the Chinese banking sector is then discussed and explained. The chapter concludes by examining the impact competition has on the risk-taking behaviour of Chinese banks. Apart from using the three competition indicators just mentioned, three different risk indicators are utilized to check the robustness of the results: the ratio of loan loss provision over total loans, the Z-score, and stability inefficiency.

Findings using the Panzar–Rosse H-statistic indicate that the Chinese banking sector operates under monopolistic competition – one of the four categories of competition; however, it is very near to perfect competition. Competition in the Chinese banking sector can by and large be attributed to Chinese banking reforms, such as the injection of capital into

SOCBs by the government, writing off the non-performing loans of SOCBs by four asset management companies, the initial public offerings of SOCBs and JSCBs, the removal of business restrictions from foreign financial institutions, and the 2008 Olympic Games held in Beijing.

Apart from estimating the competitive condition of the Chinese banking sector on a year-by-year basis, this chapter also estimates the competitive condition of the different ownerships of Chinese banks over the examined period (2003–11; Figure 5.2a). The Lerner index shows that JSCBs had lower market power (greater competition) than SOCBs and CCBs over this period. There were two reasons for this: (1) unlike SOCBs and CCBs, which are mainly funded by central or local government, JSCBs are made up of state-owned enterprises and foreign banks that are more concerned about performance, which leads to stronger competition; (2) compared with SOCBs and CCBs, which mainly grant loans to larger state-owned enterprises and small local enterprises, JSCBs primarily grant loans to small and medium-sized enterprises, which accounts for more than 90 percent of total enterprises in China. This leads to banks competing with each other to get business from these enterprises. For most years between 2003 and 2011, the competition between SOCBs was higher than that between CCBs. This can be explained by SOCBs competing with each other for business from large state-owned enterpises all over the country while CCBs primarily serve local small enterprises.

Findings on the impact competition has on the risk-taking behaviour of Chinese banks suggest that Chinese commercial banks normally have a higher volume of loan loss provision when competition is greater. This can be explained by Chinese commercial banks in a more competitive environment normally reducing credit requirements to increase the volume of business, which leads to an increase in the volume of loan loss provision.

The findings further argue that banks that are larger in terms of total assets normally have a lower volume of loan loss provision. The reason for this is that larger banks normally have greater experience of risk management and are better able to manage it. Furthermore, the risks facing large SOCBs are substantially reduced by government policies such as capital injections and non-performing loan write-offs. The findings show that Chinese commercial banks with higher levels of overhead costs normally have a higher volume of loan loss provision.

The findings show that Chinese commercial banks that are larger in terms of total assets are normally more stable, as reflected by the higher Z-score. Compared with CCBs, SOCBs and JSCBs are larger in terms of total assets. The greater stability of SOCBs can be explained by government support given in the form of capital injections and non-performing loan write-offs. It can also be explained by the government considering them too big to fail. The higher stability of JSCBs can be explained by the mixed ownerships of these banking groups. Shares held by foreign banks in JSCBs have had the effect of increasing the ability and experience of JSCBs at risk management, leading to this banking group's risk being reduced and its stability improved. The findings further argue that Chinese commercial banks with higher levels of overhead costs are normally more stable, as reflected by the higher Z-score.

The findings reported in this chapter demonstrate the need for government policies to be put in place so that the risk-taking behaviour of Chinese banks can be reduced: (1) the Chinese government and the banking regulatory authority should encourage small banks (CCBs) to merge, and in this way bank size will increase and bank stability improve; (2) the managers of Chinese commercial banks should further improve their ability to control overhead costs; (3) relevant policies should be put in place by the the Chinese government to keep inflation at a certain level.

Notes

1. The intermediation approach regards deposits as inputs and loans and investments as outputs.
2. "Charter value" is the value reflected in the share price of a bank's ability to continue to trade in the future.

6

Further development in the Chinese banking sector

Abstract: Chapters 4 and 5 focussed on using real statistics to analyze the performance and competitive condition of Chinese banking between 2003 and 2011. The impact risk has on performance and competition has on the risk-taking behaviour of Chinese banks were examined. These two chapters provided a general overview of the Chinese banking sector over the past few years. More important, however, is the future development of the Chinese banking sector – an issue that attracts great attention from the Chinese government, the banking regulatory authority, practitioners, and academic researchers. This chapter discusses the future development of the Chinese banking sector and focusses on such areas as setting up a fair and equitable salary system, internationalization, the growth of urbanization, capital replenishment, maintaining and improving innovative capacity, and implementing the Basel III capital accord.

Key words: Chinese banking, stimulation, internationalization, capitalization, urbanization, innovation.

Setting up a fair and equitable salary system

Bank efficiency measures a bank's ability to use a certain number of inputs to maximize output production or minimize the inputs to obtain a certain amount of output. As discussed in Chapter 4, inefficiency in the Chinese banking sector can largely be laid at the door of pure technical inefficiency rather than scale inefficiency. In other words, Chinese banks need to increase their ability to allocate inputs and outputs more appropriately in banking to improve efficiency. Furthermore, the results show that the efficiency of state-owned commercial banks (SOCBs) in China is substantially higher than that of joint stock commercial banks (JSCBs) and city commercial banks (CCBs). Thus, finding a way of improving the efficiency of Chinese commercial banks – especially JSCBs and CCBs – is the main focus of the Chinese government and the banking regulatory authority.

The future development of the Chinese banking industry depends on the Chinese government and the banking regulatory authority coming up with relevant policies to reduce banking input, increase output production, and by so doing improve the efficiency of Chinese banks. Banking inputs/costs mainly comprise two parts: interest expenses and non-interest expenses. Interest expenses refers to the interest paid to depositors for their deposits, the amount of which is determined by the interest rate and the size of deposits held by the banks. On the other hand, non-interest expenses can mainly be broken down into personnel expenses and other operating expenses. Personnel expenses refer to the salaries paid to staff working at the bank, while other operating expenses mainly include tax paid by the bank together with other expenses related to the operation and maintenance of facilities, equipment, furniture, and vehicles.

On 20 July 2013, under approval of the State Council, the central bank of China – the People's Bank of China (PBC) – announced that regulation regarding the loan interest rate in the Chinese banking sector was to be removed. In other words, the loan interest rate could now be determined by commercial banks themselves. Before that, the loan interest rate in China was determined by the central bank. Called the "base loan interest rate", it was used by commercial banks to adjust their own loan interest rate within certain ranges determined by the central bank.

Salaries paid to staff and management personnel constitute a major part of the non-interest expenses in banking. The annual financial statements of banks regarding the salaries of management personnel in Chinese commercial banks show that there are substantial differences between the salaries paid to management personnel at SOCBs and JSCBs. Taking 2010 as an example, the average annual salary after tax for the directors of the five SOCBs was more than RMB1 million. However, the annual salary of directors of Chinese JSCBs was substantially higher. More specifically, the highest annual salaries in Chinese commercial banks was given to the director of Shenzhen Development Bank (Ping An Bank), who was paid an annual salary of more than RMB8.25 million. Next was the director of Minsheng Bank who earned an annual salary of more than RMB7.15 million. The annual salaries of the directors of Industrial Bank and Hua Xia Bank were more than RMB3 million and RMB2.6 million, respectively. In short, the substantially higher salaries paid by JSCBs dramatically increased their non-interest expenses, which partly explains their having the lowest efficiency of commercial banks in China. Not only is there a substantial difference in the annual salary paid to directors at SOCBs and JSCBS, but the annual salary of staffs working at these banks show big differences too. More specifically, the highest salaries paid to SOCB staff were at Bank of Communication, where the average salary was RMB171,200. The next highest salaries were paid at Bank of China, Industrial and Commercial Bank of China, and China Construction Bank, where annual salaries were RMB158,300, RMB156,200, and RMB153,200, respectively. Among SOCBs, annual staff salary was lowest at Agricultural Bank of China, which paid RMB137,800.

Staff working at JSCBs are paid substantially higher annual salaries than at SOCBs. Among JSCBs, the staff at Pudong Development Bank were paid on average RMB354,700, the highest annual salaries in 2010; in second place was Hua Xia Bank, where staff annual salary was RMB353,500. Next came Minsheng Bank, where staff annual salary was RMB343,500. Staff at Everbright Bank and Merchant Bank had annual salaries of more than RMB300,000, while staff at Industrial Bank and Citic Bank were relatively lower at RMB238,000 and RMB273,000, respectively. It can be seen that even the lowest salaries paid in JSCBs were higher than the highest paid to staff at SOCBs. This substantially higher level of annual salary paid to staff at JSCBs increases non-interest expenses and is one of the reasons for their lower efficiency.

The difference between salaries paid to directors at SOCBs and JSCBs can largely be attributed to the different historical backgrounds of these two ownerships of Chinese commercial banks. On the one hand, the purpose of establishing SOCBs was to fulfill the economic plan initiated by the government and to support infrastructure construction rather than pursuing profit maximization. Up until SOCBs offered their initial public offerings on stock exchanges, the Chinese government took different measures to improve asset quality such as capital injections and non-performing loans write-offs. As a result of this historic background, the operational performance of SOCBs depends not only on market competition, but also government support. The appointment of directors in SOCBs is determined by central government, which focusses on administering specific enterprises rather than on the everyday experience of bank operation and promoting bank performance. These are the reasons there is little relationship between the annual salaries of directors and the operational performance of the bank. The performance-based part of salaries accounts for a small proportion of total salaries, hence their salaries are substantially lower than those of directors working at JSCBs.

In stark contrast, the establishment and development of JSCBs is largely based on their own activities and market competition. These activities involve them taking higher operational costs and risks, but as a result of continuously seeking new business they accumulate a higher quality of customer. Therefore, JSCBs have much stronger competitive power in Chinese banking, more innovative organizational structures, and flexible but volatile operational modes. Compared with SOCBs, the appointment of staff at JSCBs is chosen by market competition – not by the government. The directors of JSCBs play a vital role in the banks' development because they are solely responsible for taking correct decisions and setting up strategic arrangements. As a result of the formation of an effective salary stimulation system, higher salaries are awarded to directors when bank performance improves. Thus, the directors of JSCBs are paid substantially higher salaries than their counterparts in SOCBs.

Apart from bank performance, the risk/stability of the Chinese banking sector has been paid great attention by the Chinese government and the banking regulatory authority. This was in response to the 2007 financial crisis. The issue of non-performing loans, the main indicator of credit risk, is historical in the Chinese banking industry and particularly serious in Chinese SOCBs. Despite the volumes of non-performing loans in the Chinese banking sector continuing to decrease between 2003 and 2011 (as discussed in Chapter 2), it can clearly be seen that this group of commercial banks is still burdened by a larger amount of non-performing loans than any other bank ownership. The large volumes of non-performing loans in SOCBs can be partly attributed to government support, which has the effect of reducing managerial efforts to monitor and manage risk carefully. More importantly, it is closely related to the behaviour of bank managers. In other words, bank managers put their own interests first at the expense of bank stability. Managers in these banks deliberately grant loans to enterprises whose performance is lower and whose probability of loan default is higher. In return, bank managers are given bribes by these enterprises. This is the second reason for SOCBs buiding up large volumes of non-performing loans.

The bribery issue in Chinese banking dates back to the 1990s. Xuebing Wang, who was the director of Bank of China between 1995 and 1999 and became the director of China Construction Bank in 2000, received bribes worth RMB1.15 million between 1995 and 2001. After Xuebing Wang was exposed and disgraced, Enzhao Zhang took the helm as director of China Construction Bank. Between 2000 and 2004, he received bribes worth RMB4 million. In 2005, the former vice president of Bank of China, Jinbao Liu, received bribes worth RMB1.43 million. Managers in SOCBs have clearly not learnt the lessons, for bribery continues to occur. In 2012, the former vice president of Agricultural Bank of China, Kun Wang, took bribes, the actual amount of which has not been disclosed.

Since the government continues to control SOCB operation, managers and staff lack an effective salary-related stimulation system. A problem with Chinese SOCBs and JSCBs is that short-term stimulation policies are given greater emphasis than long-term stimulation policies. There are two types of short-term stimulation policy: positive and negative. They both relate staff salaries to performance. More specifically, staff salaries are the product of their performance plus a specific royalty rate. The royalty rate is normally very high under a positive short-term stimulation policy, the purpose of which is to stimulate staff to work harder and maximize their performance. Another form of positive short-term stimulation policy is to link staff performance with their welfare. For example, those members of staff who are awarded extra bonus as a result of their performance may also have the chance to travel abroad at the expense of the company and may have longer holidays than others.

On the other hand, the negative short-term stimulation policy takes on a number of forms. For instance, those members of staff whose performance is at the other end of the scale will be awarded a lower royalty rate. Some firms quite simply sack employees whose performance is low. This kind of stimulation policy puts a lot of pressure on staff and has a significant and negative impact on their health. As discussed above, there is a big difference in the salaries paid to management personnel and staff. In particular, back-room staff with little customer contact will have very low salaries compared with their front-room counterparts. This huge difference in salaries results in staff questioning the fairness of the system and further leads to a deterioration in bank efficiency. The stability of banking requires all members of staff to pull together and the enthusiasm of all members of staff to be protected. However, whereas some staff have a very good customer base and the ability to earn higher-than-usual salaries, some other staff who spend more time catering to the needs of customers may consequently have lower-than-average salaries. The difference in salary between these two groups will demotivate staff and bank efficiency will decline.

A short-term stimulation policy has little value for the long-term development of a bank, and has a negative impact on the economic growth of the country; hence the need to reform short-term stimulation policies to get rid of their limitations. First, there are a couple of postulates any reform of a stimulation policy should be based on: the efficiency-as-priority principle and the consideration-of-fairness principle. Commercial banks are profitable institutions, but the way in which they operate should follow the rules under which a market economy operates. The policy should abide by the principle of rewarding staff with higher ability and have the development of commercial banks as its target. Such a policy would require commercial banks to operate on the efficiency-as-priority principle. On the other hand, commercial banks are made up of different departments, all of whose staff contribute to the development of commercial banks. Thus, every staff member plays an important role in the development and growth of commercial banks. Apart from giving staff with greater ability higher rewards, benefits for all other staff should be given careful consideration as well. In other words, commercial banks should comply with the consideration-of-fairness principle.

Second, commercial banks need to come up with a long-term stimulation policy; in other words, a policy based on the match-performance-with-risk principle. Commercial banks should focus on the performance growth arising from a long-term stimulation policy rather than from a short-term stimulation policy. For instance, loans made by staff are a vital part of a bank's income and, hence, relevant rewards need to be given to staff with the necessary skills to attract loan business. However, commercial banks by and large fail to consider whether the loans will be repaid. In other words, they ignore the quality of the loan portfolio. It is recommended that commercial banks delay bonus payments to management and staff whose activities have a bearing on bank risk. Since commercial bank risk normally lags bonus payments to staff, delaying such payments will reduce bank risk to the extent that, should higher losses be incurred (i.e., large volume of non-performing loans), staff bonuses can be reduced or completely eliminated to cover the losses. The reason for delaying bonus payments is to steady the risk-taking behaviour of managers and contribute to the healthy development of commercial banks.

Internationalization

In 2012 the five SOCBs together with China Merchant Bank and China Development Bank continued to push their internationalization strategies. Two SOCBs – Industrial and Commercial Bank of China and Bank of China – developed their international network earlier than the other banks and gradually improved the range of their overseas business activities. Although the other three SOCBs – China Construction Bank, Agricultural Bank of China, and Bank of Communication – engaged in international business at a later time, they put greater effort into developing their overseas network. The internationalization policy pursued by China Development Bank was focussed on supporting domestic enterprises expanding their business activities overseas and, in so doing, the bank has become the largest in China for international investment and financing.

When Chinese banks first internationalized the focus of their business was the domestic market (i.e., Chinese customers), but gradually this has changed to establishing good relationships and providing services to customers in overseas markets. Major efforts have been made by large Chinese banks to acquire and upgrade banking business licences while still emphasizing the desire to expand their retail banking networks. Nowadays, Chinese banks have greater competitive power than local banks when it comes to service provision for local customers. For instance, the profit earned by Industrial and Commercial Bank of China on its overseas business activities in 2012 increased by 21.8 per cent compared with 2011, and the income earned from overseas operations accounted for 4.3

per cent of total operational income. Furthermore, the overseas assets of the bank reached USD162.7 billion at the end of 2012, which accounted for 5.8 per cent of the bank's total assets, an increase of 30.5 per cent over the previous year.

The internationalization of Chinese banks promotes the internationalization of China's official currency, the renminbi (RMB). In return, the internationalization of the RMB stimulates the internationalization of Chinese banks. The speed of RMB internationalization in recent years has accelerated, with rapid growth focussed on offshore RMB, the offshore bond market, and cross-border RMB direct investment. Hong Kong is the largest offshore RMB centre where trade settlements had increased more than 30 per cent at the end of 2012 over the previous year. Furthermore, China Development Bank has become the largest financial institution in overseas financing with its foreign currency loan balance reaching USD210.0 billion at the end of 2011.

An internationalized capital structure, trade, and investment are prerequisites to internationalization of Chinese commercial banks. The efforts made to localize overseas business activities gradually and at the same time integrate global operations contribute to Chinese bank internationalization. Since overseas exchanges have strict requirements on corporate governance and information disclosure, listings on overseas stock markets play important roles in promoting the global expansion of Chinese commercial banks. China has been increasing its participation in overseas markets, as it evolves from providing trade services to investment services. Furthermore, overseas branches have been expanded to become regional networks. More importantly, Chinese banks, which normally used to limit themselves to providing credit financing and trade settlement services for Chinese-owned enterprises, now focus on providing financial services to local customers as well.

Chinese commercial banks are expected to continue penetrating foreign markets by further developing RMB internationalization. This process will largely be attributed to increased numbers of transactions in RMB offshore settlements. In addition, Chinese commercial banks will also focus on overseas mergers and acquisitions as a result of their overseas networks expanding, and special attention will be given to developing entities with greater potential to grow. Finally, it is expected that there will be an increasing number of Chinese commercial banks seeking retail business licenses to increase their market share in providing services to local customers and further improving the localization of their overseas operations.

Growth of urbanization

China's urbanization has accelerated in recent years. Since China's economic growth is starting to slow, urbanization takes on greater importance in expanding domestic demand. The rate of urbanization in China was 52.27 per cent at the end of 2012, while the average annual growth rate of urbanization in China was 1.37 per cent between 2002 and 2012. The Chinese government is expected to spend more on construction projects to support urbanization. In 2013 Xi JinPing was elected the new president of China at the 12th National People's Congress, as were other members of the government. China will put extra effort into urbanization, which is believed to be the most effective way of expanding domestic demand and supporting overall economic stability.

China's policy of urbanization represented an opportunity for China's commercial banks. Urbanization in China has dramatically increased the volume of business engaged in by Chinese commercial banks, urbanization policies have brought about cluster development, and infrastructure construction in small and medium-sized cities has led to greater financial demand. Chinese commercial banks are the main institutions providing funds in key strategic industries such as energy, transportation, telecommunication, healthcare, cultural and mass media, and real estate. Urbanization acts not only to increase the business activities of Chinese commercial banks, it has also helped develop the branch network of Chinese commercial banks, as is evidenced by the growing number of branches in small and medium-sized cities. Apart from the increasing number of branches and larger volumes of business engaged in by Chinese banks, Chinese commercial banks are expected to put greater resources into developing payment systems by popularizing the use of bank cards and setting up more ATMs in small towns and cities and more bank card machines in shops. Efforts are also expected to be made to promote innovative payment transactions like online payments, phone payments, and mobile payments.

Chinese commercial banks have also developed and strengthened their collaboration with government agencies in providing support for China's urbanization. For instance, private enterprise and collective economy were introduced as a result of collaboration between China Development Bank and local government, enterprises with different ownership forms were created, and suburban development funds were established to support infrastructure development. What is more, by collaborating with the government at the province level Agricultural Bank of China increased its self-service outlets in Guangdong by 1,000 – a further expansion of its branch network. In addition, Agricultural Bank of China increased the number of its Golden Spike Cards as part of the Huinongtong Project by 10,000. This provides a means of connecting urban and rural areas through a convenient and fast financial service network.

The extensive branch network that has been developed, together with the increased use of different payment facilities and methods to meet the requirements of Chinese urbanization, will significantly promote the development of Chinese commercial banks. The National Development and Reform Commission published the *National Planning for Promoting Healthy Urbanization (2011–2012)*. This document states that more than RMB40 trillion is expected to be invested for China's urbanization. Such a large demand for funds provides room for China's commercial banks to expand. At the moment, government bonds are the main means of financing urbanization in China. Government bonds are considered to be the best means of financing urbanization – certainly better than bank loans – because the maturity of government bonds is longer, which sums up the time infrastructure construction in China is expected to take.

Chinese commercial banks are expected in the future to increase their ability to finance China's urbanization. They are expected to come up with more effective products and services. Furthermore, Chinese commercial banks are expected to provide more support to small-sized enterprises by offering them comprehensive financial services such as lending, investment, insurance, and leasing.

Capital replenishment

The China Banking Regulatory Commission (CBRC) published the *Capital Management Measures of Commercial Banks* (hereinafter referred to as "the new rules"). The new rules were implemented in January 2013 and had a number of purposes: they reflected the Basel III regulatory capital requirement, set out the minimum capital adequacy ratio (CAR) requirement for commercial banks, and provided detailed guidelines on calculating capital and risk-weighted assets. Currently, Chinese commercial banks use three main channels to replenish capital: (1) retained earnings, (2) issuing common shares, and (3) issuing subordinated bonds. These capital replenishment methods are believed to have relatively higher cost.

Chongqing Rural Commercial Bank successfully made its IPO in 2010. However, it took more than two years for additional Chinese commercial banks to get listed. The Chinese government is expected to introduce stricter regulations on domestic IPOs. Since all SOCBs and many JSCBs have already got themselves listed on stock exchanges, the public listings of small commercial banks (city and rural banks) represent a major issue for the Chinese government and the Banking Regulatory Authority. However, the Banking Regulatory Authority has not promulgated the guidelines governing the IPOs of small commercial banks and, thus, the IPO process of these banks has been delayed. There are a number of commercial banks planning to get listed. This has attracted a great deal of attention from the general public. For example, Bank of Shanghai plans to get listed on the Hong Kong Stock Exchange; Bank of Chongqing plans to get listed on both the Hong Kong and Shanghai stock exchanges; after making its IPO on the Shanghai Stock Exchange, China Everbright plans to get listed on the Hong Kong Stock Exchange; and Guangdong Development Bank and Huishang Bank also have plans to make their IPOs.

Apart from issuing common shares to replenish capital, China's commercial banks also issue subordinate bonds. Since the requirement regarding the CAR specified in the new rules was higher than before, China's commercial banks issued subordinate bonds in 2012 to increase capital levels and, in so doing, meet the requirement. By the end of 2012 the number of subordinate bonds issued by Chinese commercial banks reached 33 with a value of more than RMB224 billion. The rate offered was 8.1 per cent.

Apart from issuing common shares and subordinate bonds, non-governmental investment plays an important role in increasing the capital levels of Chinese commercial banks. In an effort to get non-governmental organization to invest in China's commercial banks and further restructure China's rural and urban credit cooperatives, "several opinions regarding to encourage and guide the sound development of non-governmental capital" were put forward by the State Council in 2010. The result has been a growing volume of non-government capital invested in Chinese banking in the last couple of years, especially in city and rural commercial banks. This capital has been used to restructure and reform these banks. Capital injection from non-governmental organizations not only increases the capital levels of Chinese commercial banks, it helps banks expand their business activities, enhance their risk management, and improve their governance structures.

On 7 December 2012, the *Guidance of the Innovation of Capital Instruments of the Commercial Banks* was published by the CBRC. Not only does this publication outline the basic principles to be followed when making capital instruments more innovative, the relevant policies needed to regulate the development of capital instruments are also provided. Furthermore, the publication clearly sets out policies relating to the expansion of capital replenishment. In April 2013 China's commercial banks were encouraged to develop capital instruments. They were also encouraged to use different channels to increase capital levels. The CBRC focusses on the issuance of two kinds of new capital instruments: secondary capital instruments[1] with write-down features and equity capital instruments with relevant departments.[2] Implementation of the guidance has resulted in innovative new capital instruments being developed and Chinese commercial banks discovering new channels to increase capital levels. Twelve Chinese listed banks passed capital bills at the annual meetings of shareholders/board of directors. Capital instruments and subordinate bonds worth more than RMB360 billion are expected to be issued over the next three years.

The capital replenishment of Chinese commercial banks is expected to develop significantly in the future. The new rules allow Chinese commercial banks to use different channels to increase capital levels. The number of listed channels to do this is limited. The issue is further complicated by the likelihood of the Chinese government imposing stricter regulatory barriers on bank IPOs. Thus, increasing numbers of Chinese commercial banks are looking to get themselves listed abroad. Furthermore, the government is expected to continue to support the capital participation of non-governmental organizations in Chinese commercial banks because not only will the capital levels of commercial banks increase, but it will play an important role in reforming and restructuring small commercial banks.

As far as innovation in capital investment is concerned, two kinds of capital investments are expected to be issued: (1) secondary capital instruments with write-down features and (2) equity capital instruments with relevant departments.

Upgrading innovation capacity

Currently, the focus of Chinese commercial banks is still on making loans to medium and large-sized enterprises. However, increased competition together with market-oriented interest rate reform and increased pressure on capital levels have made Chinese commercial banks rethink and expand their business scope. The new areas of business that Chinese commercial banks are focussing on include asset securitization, the financing of micro and small-sized enterprises, data and core application improvement, mobile payments, and Internet finance.

Asset securitization in China stagnated as a result of the 2007 financial crisis. But in May 2012, when the *Notice on Relevant Matters Concerning Further Expanding the Pilot Securitization of Credit Assets* was published by the People's Bank of China, the CBRC, and the Ministry of Finance, it was reintroduced. This has brought huge business opportunities for commercial banks. Chinese commercial banks are currently making major strides toward this kind of business innovation because of the profitability it brings. In the coming years, there will be gradual improvement in capital release, risk spreading, and asset adjusting as a result of business securitization being developed. But, first, there needs to be well-organized and sustainable development of Chinese commercial banks as a result of coordinated development of product innovation, accounting, information disclosure, institutional training and regulation. Currently, business securitization only focuses on quality assets. As a consequence Chinese banks and regulatory authorities are expected to increase their risk control and management capabilities, especially after asset securitization is fully liberated.

Until very recently, it was very difficult for micro and small-sized enterprises in China to get funds. There was a need for the financial products and services of Chinese commercial banks to be much more innovative and for these banks to switch their focus to providing finance for micro and small-sized enterprises in China. It was believed the provision of fundamental support to these enterprises would not only promote their growth and development but also help Chinese commercial banks build competitive advantages. By increasing the volumes of finance to micro and small-sized enterprises the high concentration of banking loans to medium and large-sized enterprises in the overall banking loan portfolio would be significantly reduced, and by making loans available to all types of enterprises the economic development of the country as a whole would benefit. The volume of business undertaken by banks to finance micro and small-sized enterprises in China has grown in recent years. More specifically, the value of loans granted by Chinese commercial banks to micro and small-sized enterprises reached RMB14.8 trillion at the end of 2012, accounting for 28.6 per cent of total loans. The growth rate of loans to micro and small-sized enterprises was 2.6 per cent higher than that of total loans. Chinese commercial banks are expected to put more effort into making future products and services for micro and small-sized enterprises much more innovative. The areas recommended for Chinese commercial banks to focus on are market positioning, acquisition of quality clients, integration of products and channels, and reform of internal management systems.

Chinese banks are investing more in the area of information technology (IT) and commercial banks are paying greater attention to managing big data.[3] The more IT and its secure operation develop the greater the impact on the stability and reputation of bank, resulting in greater financial and social stability. This is the reason Chinese commercial banks are spending more on building and developing IT. The downside is that the growth rate of spending exceeds that of profitability. Banks that are better at data analysis are believed to be better positioned to satisfy customers. Chinese commercial banks are expected in the coming years to invest more on managing and analysing big data, to spend more on technical instruments that will supposedly help them get better at risk management, and to concentrate more on client analysis and, by doing so, provide guidance on business development. Products and services can be adjusted and optimized for individual customer satisfaction as a result of analysing comprehensive information about clients, such as information on consumption, credit, preference, and behaviour.

Mobile payments and online banking have significantly developed in recent years in China. China UnionPay is the only domestic bank card organization and the only interbank network in the country (excluding Hong Kong and Macau); it promotes mobile payments. TSMs (trusted service managers) have been set up; they act as neutral brokers between financial institutions and mobile operators. The first group of commercial banks using the TSM platform included China Citic Bank, Bank of China, Shanghai Pudong Development Bank, Guangdong Development Bank, China Everbright Bank, and Postal Savings Bank of China. As was the case with mobile payments, the number of customers using online banking has increased significantly in recent years. As technology has improved and regulatory policies liberalized, the digital channels of financial services have become competitors of the traditional channels of providing financial services. Chinese commercial banks are expected in the coming years to integrate and coordinate these two channels with the objectives of improving customer experience, increasing bank competitive power, and promoting bank performance.

Implementation of Basel III Capital Accord

Basel I focussed on credit risk and appropriate risk weighting of assets. It required banks with an international presence to hold capital equal to 8 per cent of their risk-weighted assets. Basel II differed from Basel I by creating an international standard that banking regulators could use to control how much capital banks needed to set aside for the financial and operational risks that they faced. Basel III is the result of ongoing efforts by the Basel Committee on Banking Supervision. It builds on Basel I and Basel II and focusses on strengthening bank capital requirements by increasing bank liquidity and decreasing bank leverage. The new rules mentioned in the section on "Capital replenishment" have stricter requirements for the CAR of commercial banks. The core Tier 1 capital ratio, Tier 1 capital ratio, and CAR should be at least 7.5, 8.5, and 10.5 per cent, respectively, while all these figures are increased by 1 per cent for domestic banks. In other words, domestic banks should make sure that their core Tier 1 capital ratio, Tier 1 capital ratio, and CAR are no less than 8.5, 9.5, and 11.5 per cent, respectively. Losses and financial instability are dealt with by capital instruments that are used to increase the capital levels of Chinese commercial banks, which are clearly defined by the CBRC.

The new rules formulated by the CBRC play important roles in increasing the capital levels of Chinese commercial banks and improving asset quality. Since 2010 China's economic growth has slowed, as reflected by the annual GDP growth rate, and as a result asset quality is expected to be influenced. Chinese commercial banks are regulated to keep higher levels of capitalization to deal with unexpected losses. The average CAR and core Tier 1 CAR of the Chinese banking sector at the end of 2012 reached 13.25 and 10.62 per cent, respectively, while the capital levels of the five SOCBs were even higher than that at a CAR of 13.66 per cent and a core Tier 1 CAR of 10.68 per cent. Some small and medium-sized JSCBs, city commercial banks, and rural commercial banks have not met the capital requirement – a problem the entire Chinese banking sector has to address.

Chinese commercial banks are expected to fully implement the new rules formulated by the CBRC in the next few years. They will engage in capital planning and stress testing to establish longer term capital mechanisms and increase the efficiency of planned capital management. They will also focus on expanding the channels used for capital replenishment in an effort to reduce financing costs and increase the flexibility of contingency plans.

As a response to the new rules, Chinese commercial banks have taken a number of measures to reform the way they operate. For instance, risk measurement models, policy streams, and information systems have been established by large national commercial banks, which have applied the models to bank daily business and risk management. Moreover, the collateral management systems, model laboratories, and risk data warehouses of these banks have also been upgraded and great steps have been taken toward improving capital management capabilities. Chinese commercial banks are focussed on establishing and improving advanced quantitative risk assessment methods. The two approaches used by banks to bring this about are: the advanced internal ratings approach of credit risk and the advanced evaluation approach of operational risk.

The situation with JSCBs is similar. Some have already met the capital requirements specified by the Capital Accord; others have submitted assessment applications, which are currently being assessed by the CBRC; and yet others are making efforts to meet the capital requirements via a variety of means (e.g., reforming the government structure, improving the management process, and upgrading calculation instruments and data systems).

Conclusion

This chapter discusses how Chinese banking is expected to develop over the next few years. The discussion focusses on areas like setting up a fair and equitable salary system, the internationalization of Chinese banks, the impact urbanization growth has on Chinese banks, capital replenishment, upgrading the innovative capacity of Chinese banks, and implementation of the Basel III Capital Accord. As far as setting up a fair and equitable salary system is concerned, it is argued that the short-term stimulation policies currently implemented by the Chinese banking sector have an adverse effect on bank development and negatively impact the economic growth of the whole country. A stimulation policy should be based on a couple of postulates: the efficiency-as-priority principle and the consideration-of-fairness principle. The chapter recommends higher rewards/ benefits should be allocated to staff members who are more efficient or more capable. However, it is important to keep in mind that bank development is achieved as a result of the efforts of all the staff from the various departments – not just the front-room staff. The huge difference of rewards between staff members will significantly reduce the efforts of staff at the other end of the pay scale. A similar situation arises when – as is commonly the case – senior staff are paid substantially higher salaries than other staff members. Reducing the amount paid to senior staff will not only create a relatively fairer environment, it will also reduce bank costs and further improve bank efficiency, although it runs the risk of senior staff moving to other banks. The chapter further recommends that banks should match performance with risk and focus on the quality of loan business rather than the volume of loans made by staff. Since risk lags bonus payments, it is recommended that banks delay bonus payments to staff whose activities affect the risk condition of the bank in question. This will reduce the risk-taking behaviour of staff and decrease bank costs.

Expectations concerning Chinese bank internationalization are that Hong Kong, as the largest offshore RMB centre, will continue to play a vital role in promoting RMB internationalization for the foreseeable future, and that Chinese commercial banks will change their focus to mergers and acquisitions. In addition, an increasing number of commercial banks are expected to obtain retail business licenses allowing them to penetrate local markets and further improve the localization of overseas operations. Chinese banks are also expected to participate in China's urbanization and benefit from the business opportunities that would bring. The specific focus of Chinese commercial banks should be the introduction of effective products and services, especially the provision of comprehensive financial services, such as lending, investment, insurance, and leasing, to small-sized enterprises in China.

Chinese commercial banks are expected to use different channels in the coming years to increase capital levels and, as a result of the stringent restriction on banks IPOs imposed by the Chinese banking regulatory authority, more and more Chinese commercial banks are expected to be listed on overseas exchanges. It is further expected that capital invested by non-governmental organizations in China's commercial banks will continue to increase, and that second capital instruments with write-down features and equity capital instruments with relevant departments will be the two main innovative capital investments in future years.

As far as upgrading the innovative capacity of Chinese commercial banks is concerned, the expectation is that they will focus on devising innovative products and services for micro and small-sized enterprises, and more effort will be put into market positioning, acquisition of quality clients, integration of products and channels, and reform of internal management systems. They are also expected to concentrate on analysing comprehensive information about clients such as information on consumption, credit, preference, and behaviour as a means of improving the customer experience.

China's commercial banks are expected to better integrate and coordinate the traditional and digital channels used to provide financial products and services in an effort to improve customer satisfaction and bank performance. Implementation of the new rules formulated by the CBRC is expected to be completed by China's commercial banks, which will be achieved by capital planning and stress testing. Finally, capital replenishment channels are expected to be expanded.

Notes

1. Secondary capital instruments with write-down features are also called Tier 2 capital instruments with write-down terms (i.e., write-down bonds). A write-down bond is bank capital that can be used for loss absorption in case of unsustainable operation.
2. Equity instruments with relevant departments relates to commercial banks strengthening research into regulations, policies and markets; communicating and coordinating with investors and relevant departments; creating a friendly external environment for capital instrument innovation; and actively exploring ways to issue various new-type capital instruments via different markets.
3. "Big data" can be defined as personal information about our individual preferences gathered by brands and marketers that is then used to target ads at us; despite being invasive it can make life easier.

7

Conclusion

Abstract: This chapter summarizes the book's empirical findings and looks in particular at the effects risk has on bank performance and competition has on the risk-taking behaviour of Chinese banks. In addition to empirical results, relevant explanations are given. The chapter then discusses the policy implications of the findings, which hopefully will be found useful for government officials, banking regulatory authorities, bank managers and practitioners, as well as academic researchers. Finally, this chapter outlines how the author envisages the future development of the Chinese banking industry.

Key words: summary, findings, risk and performance, competition and risk, policy iplications, future development.

Introduction and summary of findings

The banking sector in China has played an important role in the country's economic development. Over the last 30 years, the Chinese government has initiated several rounds of banking reforms and the banking sector has undergone significant changes. The reforms had the purposes of improving performance, increasing competition, and enhancing stability in the banking sector. This book investigates the performance, competition conditions, and risk conditions between 2003 and 2011. A particular focus of the book is bank performance, especially bank technical efficiency/productivity and bank profitability. More importantly, the book empirically tests the impact risk has on bank performance (bank profitability, efficiency, and productivity) and the effect competition has on the risk-taking behaviour of Chinese banks.

As just mentioned, the series of banking reforms initiated by the Chinese government in the late 1970s had three main objectives: to improve performance, increase competitive conditions, and build a safe and stable banking sector. Before 1979, the Chinese banking sector followed the banking model of the Soviet Union. The People's Bank of China (PBC) had the dual role of acting as the central bank and engaging in commercial banking activities at the same time. The first round of banking reforms initiated by the government covered the period 1979–1992. A two-tier banking system was established during this period with the PBC free to serve as the central bank and four state-owned commercial banks (SOCBs) were set up primarily for commercial banking activities. In addition to SOCBs, a number of joint stock commercial banks (JSCBs) as well as rural and urban credit cooperatives were established during this period. The second round of banking reforms initiated by the Chinese government took place in 1993 and had the objectives of reducing government intervention in bank operations and enhancing stability in the banking sector. Before 1993, the four SOCBs were under direct control of the central government and had no power regarding credit and lending decisions. The SOCBs were purposely set up to grant loans to large state-owned enterprises under the direction of the government. However, most state-owned enterprises did not perform well. These firms had a higher probability of default and, as a consequence, SOCBs were saddled with higher volumes of non-performing loans. In an effort to overcome this problem, three policy banks were established to undertake policy-lending activities under the direction of the government. This gave SOCBs more freedom with regard to credit allocation.

The 1997 Asian financial crisis raised government concerns about risk-taking behaviour and stability in the banking sector. In response to the crisis, the government set up four asset management companies tasked with writing off the non-performing loans of SOCBs.

The third round of banking reforms took place after China joined the World Trade Organization (WTO) in December 2001. Many new measures were undertaken in this reform. For instance, the new banking regulatory authority – the China Banking Regulatory Commission (CBRC) – was established; the Chinese government provided SOCBs with equity capital; restrictions on the entry and operation of foreign banks were removed; foreigners were allowed to invest in Chinese banks; and a number of commercial banks were listed on stock exchanges. At the end of 2011 the Chinese banking sector consisted of 5 SOCBs, 12 JSCBs, 144 CCBs and a large number of other banking and non-bank financial institusions. Despite the assets of SOCBs as a proportion of total banking sector assets decreasing ever since 2003, SOCBs still dominated in the Chinese banking sector. The assets of the five SOCBs as of the end of 2011 still accounted for nearly 50 per cent of total banking sector assets.

Using information on 101 Chinese banks, this book investigates the determinants of bank profitability with particular focus given to the impact risk has on bank profitability. The four profitability measures used are return on assets (ROA), return on equity (ROE), net interest margin (NIM), and profit margin (PBT), all of which are widely applied in the literature on banking profitability. When it comes to dealing with such issues as profit persistence, endogeneity, and unobserved heterogeneity, the Generalized Method of Moments (GMM) two-step system estimator is used to investigate the impact risk has on bank profitability. There has been much empirical research investigating the determinants of bank profitability. This book contributes to this research by investigating the effect risk has on bank profitability. The author believes it is the first empirical study to measure Chinese bank risk using the Z-score and stability inefficiency and further test the impact it has had on bank profitability in China. The empirical findings suggest there is no clear evidence regarding the impact risk has had on bank profitability in China. This can be explained by the support given by the Chinese government to SOCBs to counter the higher costs incurred by their higher risk-taking behaviour. Different forms of government support have been given such as capital injection and non-performing loan write-offs, the latter through four asset management companies. The empirical results further find that Chinese bank profitability is affected by different determinants. More specifically, the findings show that large Chinese banks (in terms of total assets) are more profitable, while those banks with highly productive workforces have higher profitability. In addition, a highly concentrated banking market and well-developed banking sector have a significant and positive impact on bank profitability in China. Finally, the results reveal that when inflation is high, Chinese banks are more profitable.

Technical efficiency is another area examined by this book. Using a non-parametric data envelopment analysis (DEA) Charnes–Cooper–Rhodes (CCR) model, this book examines the technical efficiency of 101 Chinese banks beween 2003 and 2011. The results indicate that SOCBs are the most technically efficient, followed by JSCBs, while CCBs are the least technically efficient. Furthermore, the DEA Banker–Charnes–Cooper (BCC) model is used to find the sources of technical inefficiency. It is also used to investigate pure technical efficiency and scale efficiency. The findings suggest that SOCBs are the most pure technically efficient, followed by JSCBs, and CCBs are the least pure technically efficient. In addition, the efficiency scores derived from the DEA BCC model show that Chinese banks are more scale efficient than pure technically efficient, which means that Chinese commercial banks are pure technically inefficient and, hence, misallocate inputs and outputs in their banking operation.

In addition to the technical efficiency of different ownerships of Chinese banks, the book also looks at how risk impacts the efficiency of Chinese banking while controlling for comprehensive bank-specific, industry-specific, and macroeconomic determinants of bank efficiency. The results suggest that Chinese banks with lower overhead costs are more technically efficient. This finding reflects the fact that Chinese banks can be made more efficient by improving managers' ability to control overhead costs. The findings differ from those of bank profitability by showing that a more productive workforce leads to a decline in technical efficiency. This finding can be explained by banks offering higher wages to attract and retain more experienced, more productive staff. The payment of higher wages increases bank costs, which leads to a decline in bank efficiency. The results further reveal that the technical and pure technical efficiency of Chinese banks is higher in a more concentrated, highly developed banking sector. Finally, a higher GDP growth rate and inflation rate lead to a decline in bank efficiency.

The book also looks at the productivity of three different ownerships of Chinese banks. Using 2003 as the reference year and comparing the productivity indices of SOCBs, JSCBs, and CCBs from 2004 to 2011, the results indicate that SOCBs had the highest productivity growth in 2005 while CCBs had the highest productivity decline in 2007. Furthermore, all commercial banks experienced productivity growth in 2005 and productivity decline was noticed in all commercial banks in 2006. However, between 2008 and 2011 all banks experienced productivity decline, except in 2009. In the second half of the book, the impact risk has on bank productivity is tested. The results show that the impact is negligible and that Chinese banks are more productive when the banking market is less concentrated.

In addition to profitability, efficiency, and productivity, the competitive condition of Chinese banks between 2003 and 2011 is another area examined by this book. When the competitive condition is measured by the Lerner index, the results indicate that CCBs were the least competitive between 2004 and 2009, while JSCBs were the most competitive over the entire period examined. Bank competition was also measured by the three-bank concentration ratio, which shows the competitive condition of Chinese banking on a year-by-year basis. The three-bank concentration ratio reveals that competition in the Chinese banking sector remained low over the period examined and that SOCBs still dominated the Chinese banking industry. An alternative indicator of bank competition, the Panzar–Rosse H-statistic, was also used to assess the competitive condition of the Chinese banking sector. The findings suggest that the Chinese banking sector was least competitive in 2003, which can mainly be attributed to the Chinese government injecting capital into SOCBs. Government protection and support lead to a decline in bank competition. By contrast, the Chinese banking sector was most competitive in 2006, which can be explained by two SOCBs – Industrial and Commercial Bank of China and Bank of China – becoming listed. The Chinese banking sector was relatively more competitive in 2008 and 2010 than in other years, when the Panzar–Rosse H-statistic was more than 0.8. The greater competition in 2008 can be explained by the Beijing Olympic Games, while the competitive condition of the Chinese banking sector in 2010 was down to the last SOCBs getting listed and one of the biggest JSCBs – Everbright Bank – making its initial public offering.

In the second half of this book the impact competition has on the risk-taking behaviour of Chinese banks is examined. Empirical findings suggest that greater competition leads to an increase in the loan loss provisions set aside by Chinese banks. The results show that large (in terms of total assets) Chinese banks needed less in the way of loan loss provisions and that Chinese banks with higher overhead costs needed more. When risk is measured by the Z-score, the findings suggest that large (in terms of total assets) Chinese banks had lower risk. The results differ from those reported when risk is measured by the ratio of loan loss provisions over total loans in that higher overhead costs lead to lower risk-taking behaviour (higher Z-score).

Policy implications and further development of Chinese banking

This book's empirical findings point the way for future reforms in the Chinese banking sector. The policy implications of this study for the Chinese government and the banking regulatory authority relate to improvements in performance and stability of the Chinese banking sector. The policy implications of this study can be summarized as follows:

- To improve stability in the Chinese banking sector and reduce the risk-taking behaviour of Chinese banks, the Chinese government and banking regulatory authority should encourage mergers and acquisitions among small commercial banks (i.e., CCBs) – any increase in bank size will lead to an improvement in bank stability. The Chinese government and banking regulatory authority should put in place policies to improve the corporate governance of Chinese banks – in particular, an appropriate mechanism should be established to monitor the behaviour of management staff. Getting rid of bribery in all its forms in the Chinese banking sector will reduce the volume of non-performing loans and significantly improve bank stability. Finally, banking staff should be given more training in non-traditional activities. The more experienced staff are in non-traditional activities the smaller the bank's dependence on traditional loan–deposit services. Reducing the volume of loans granted by Chinese banks will increase liquidity levels and further improve stability.

- To improve performance in the Chinese banking industry, greater effort should be made to recruit staff that are more experienced and special attention should be given to provide more training and professional opportunities to existing staff, with the aim of increasing productivity and further improving bank performance. In addition, inflation should be carefully controlled for to counterbalance increases in profitability and declines in bank efficiency. SOCBs should expand their business in both traditional and non-traditional activities, the resultant increase in concentration would lead to an improvement in bank profitability and efficiency.
- To set up a future salary-related stimulation system, it is recommended that a proper stimulation policy should be established in the Chinese banking sector based on a couple of postulates: the efficiency-as-priority principle and the consideration-of-fairness principle. In addition, Chinese commercial banks should reduce the salaries/bonuses allocated to senior staff, with the objectives of creating a relatively fairer environment and reducing bank costs, which will lead to an improvement in bank

performance. Finally, it is recommended that Chinese commercial banks should match performance with risk, put more emphasis on the quality of the loan business than the quantity of loans, and delay bonus payments to staff whose activities have a major impact on the risk portfolio of banks, which should result in a substantial reduction in risk-taking behaviour.

The Chinese banking sector is expected to get much more involved in internationalization in the coming years. Hong Kong, as the largest RMB offshore centre, will keep its vital role in promoting RMB internationalization. A growing number of Chinese banks are expected to focus more on providing financial services to local markets. At the same time Chinese commercial banks are expected to participate more in urbanization, which provides huge opportunities for business expansion, and particularly concentrate on offering comprehensive financial services to small-sized enterprises. Since capitalization plays an important role in the stability of the financial sector, Chinese commercial banks are expected to use different channels to replenish capital. More commercial banks are expected to be listed on overseas exchanges because of the stringent requirements imposed by the Chinese banking regulatory authority regarding domestic bank IPOs. The capital participation of non-governmental organizations in Chinese commercial banks is expected to increase. Chinese commercial banks are expected to make use of innovative capital instruments such as secondary capital instruments with write-down features[1] or equity capital instruments with relevant departments.[2] Chinese commercial banks are expected not only to focus on making products and services provided to micro and small-sized enterprises in China more innovative, but greater attention is also expected to be given to market positioning, acquisition of quality clients, integration of products and channels, and reform of internal management systems. Customer satisfaction is expected to improve and bank performance increase as a result of analysing comprehensive information about clients and integrating and coordinating traditional and digital channels when providing financial products and services. Finally, the capital replenishment channels available to Chinese commercial banks are expected to increase and greater focus is expected to be given to capital planning and stress testing such that the capital management rules formulated by the CBRC can be implemented more effectively.

Notes

1. Secondary capital instruments with write-down features are also called Tier 2 capital instruments with write-down terms (i.e., write-down bonds). A write-down bond is bank capital that can be used for loss absorption in case of unsustainable operation.
2. Equity instruments with relevant departments relates to commercial banks strengthening research into regulations, policies and markets; communicating and coordinating with investors and relevant departments; creating a friendly external environment for capital instrument innovation; and actively exploring ways to issue various new-type capital instruments via different markets.

References

Aboody, D., and Kasznik, R. (2000) CEO Stock Option Awards and the timing of corporate voluntary disclosures. *Journal of Accounting and Economics*, **29**(1), 73–110.

Aburime, U.T. (2009) Impact of political affiliation on bank profitability in Nigeria. *African Journal of Accounting, Economics, Finance and Banking Research*, **4**, 61–75.

Agoraki, M.E., Delis, M.D., and Pasiouras, F. (2009) Regulations, competition and bank risk-taking in transition countries. *Journal of Financial Risk*, **71**(3), 38–48.

Aigner, D., Lovell, C.K., and Schmidt, P. (1977) Formulation and estimation of stochastic frontier production function models. *Journal of Econometrics*, **6**, 21–37.

Akhavein, J., Berger, A.N., and Humphrey, D.B (1997) The effects of megamergers on efficiency and prices: evidence from a bank profit function. *Review of Industrial Organization*, **12**(1), 95–139.

Akmal, M., and Saleem, M. (2008) Technical efficiency of banking sector in Pakistan. *SBP Research Bulletin*, 4, 61–79.

Alchian, A., and Demsetz, H. (1972) Production, information costs and economic organization. *American Economic Review*, **62**, 777–95.

Allen, F., and Gale, D. (2000) Financial contagion. *Journal of Political Economy*, **108**(1), 1–33.

Allen, F., and Gale, D. (2004) Competition and financial stability. *Journal of Money, Credit and Banking*, **26**(3), 453–80.

Amba, M.S., and Almukharreq, F. (2013) Impact of the financial crisis on profitability of the islamic banks vs conventional banks: evidence from GCC. *International Journal of Financial Research*, **4**, 84–93.

Antle, R., and Smith, A. (1986) An empirical investigation of the relative performance evaluation of corporate executives. *Journal of Accounting Research*, **24**, 1–39.

Arellano, M., and Bond, S.R. (1991) Some tests of specification for panel data: Monte Carlo evidence and an application to employment equations. *Review of Economic Studies*, **58**, 277–97.

Arellano, M., and Bover, O. (1995) Another look at the instrumental–variable estimation of error–components models. *Journal of Econometrics*, **68**, 29–52.

Ariff, M., and Can, L. (2008) Cost and profit efficiency of Chinese banks: a non-parametric analysis. *China Economic Review*, **19**, 260–73.

Ariss, R.T. (2010) On the implications of market power in banking: evidence from developing countries. *Journal of Banking and Finance*, **34**, 765–75.

Athanasoglou, P.P., Brissimis, S.N., and Delis, M.D. (2008) Bank-specific, industry-specific and macroeconomic determinants of bank profitability. *Journal of International Financial Markets, Institutions and Money*, **18**(2), 121–36.

Athanasoglou, P.P., Georgiou, E.A., and Staikouras, C.C. (2009) Assessing output and productivity growth in the banking industry. *Quarterly Review of Economics and Finance*, **49**, 1317–40.

Balk, B.M. (2001) Scale efficiency and productivity change. *Journal of Productivity Analysis*, **15**, 159–83.

Baltensperger, E., and Dermine, J. (1987) Banking deregulation in Europe. *Economic Policy: A European Forum*, **4**, 64–109.

Banerjee, A. (1997) A theory of misgovernance. *Quarterly Journal of Economics*, **112**, 1289–332.

Banker, R.D., Charnes, A., and Cooper, W.W. (1984) Some models for estimating technical and scale inefficiencies in Data Envelopment Analysis. *Management Science*, **30**, 1078–92.

Barro, R.J. (1999) Notes on growth accounting. *Journal of Economic Growth*, **4**, 119–37.

Barth, J.R., Caprio Jr, G., and Levine, R. (2001) *Bank Supervision and Regulation: What Works Best?* (World Bank Policy Research Working Paper No. 2725). World Bank, Washington, D.C.

Bashir, A. (2003) Determinants of profitability and rates of return margins in islamic banks: some evidence from the Middle East. *Islamic Economic Studies*, **11**(1), 31–57.

Baumol, W.J., Panzar, J.C., and Willig, R.D. (1982) *Contestable Markets and the Theory of Industry Structure*. Harcourt Brace Jovanovich, San Diego, CA.

BCBS (1998) *Framework for the Evaluation of Internal Control System*. Basel Committee on Banking Supervision, Basel, Switzerland.

Becher, D.A., Campbell, T.L., and Frye, M.B. (2005) Incentives compensation for bank directors: the impact of deregulation. *Journal of Business*, **78**(5), 1753–777.

Beck, T. (2008) *Bank Competition and Financial Stability: Friends or Foes?* (Policy Research Working Paper No. 4656). World Bank, Washington, DC.

Beck, T., Hesse, H., Kick, T., and Westernhagen, N.V. (2009) *Bank Ownership and Stability: Evidence from Germany* (Vox Working Paper No. 2009). European Union, Brussels, Belgium.

Ben Naceur, S. (2003) The determinants of the Tunisian banking industry profitability: panel evidence. Paper presented at *Economic Research Forum (ERF) Tenth Annual Conference, 16–18 December 2003.*

Berger, A.N. (1991) Market discipline in banking. *Proceedings of the Conference on Bank Structure and Competition.* Federal Reserve Bank of Chicago, pp. 419–37.

Berger, A.N (1995a) The relationship between capital and earnings in banking. *Journal of Money, Credit and Banking*, **27**, 432–56.

Berger, A.N. (1995b) The profit–structure relationship in banking: test of market power and efficient structure hypothesis. *Journal of Money, Credit and Banking*, **27**(2), 404–31.

Berger, A.N., and Udell, G. (2004) The institutional memory hypothesis and the procyclicality of bank lending behaviour. *Journal of Financial Intermediation*, **13**(4), 458–95.

Berger, A.N., Klapper, L.F., and Turk-Ariss, R. (2009) Bank competition and financial stability. *Journal of Financial Services Research*, **35**, 99–118.

Berle, A., and Means, G. (1932) *Private Property and the Corporation.* Macmillan, New York.

Bikker, J., and Hu, H. (2002) Cyclical patterns in profits, provisioning and lending of banks and procyclicality of the new Basel capital requirements. *BNL Quarterly Review*, **221**, 143–75.

Bikker, J.A., Spierdijk, L., and Finnie, P. (2007) *The Impact of Market Structure, Contestability and Institutional Environment on Bank Competition* (DNB Working Paper No. 156). De Nederlandsche Bank, Amsterdam.

Blair, M.M. (1995) *Ownership and Control: Rethinking Corporate Governance for the Twenty-first Century.* Brookings Institution, Washington, D.C.

Blum, J. (2002) Subordinated debt, market discipline, and banks' risk taking. *Journal of Banking and Finance*, **26**(7), 1427–41.

Blundell, R., and Bond, S. (1998) Initial conditions and moment restrictions in dynamic panel data model. *Journal of Econometrics*, **87**, 115–43.

Bond, S. (2002) Dynamic panel data models: a guide to micro data methods and practice. *Portuguese Economic Journal*, **1**(2), 141–62.

Boot, W.A., and Greenbaum, S. (1993) Bank regulation, reputation and rents: theory and policy implications. In: C. Mayer and X. Vives (Eds), *Capital Markets and Financial Intermediation.* Cambridge University Press, Cambridge, UK, pp. 292–318.

Bourke, P (1989) Concentration and other determinants of bank profitability in Europe, North America and Australia. *Journal of Banking and Finance*, **13**, 65–79.

Boyd, J.H., and De Nicolo, G. (2005) The theory of bank risk taking and competition revisited. *Journal of Finance*, **60**, 1329–43.

Boyd, J.H., De Nicolo, G., and Jalal, A.M. (2006) *Bank Risk Taking and Competition Revisited: New Theory and Evidence* (Working Paper No. 06/29). International Monetary Fund, Washington, DC.

Buch, C.M., Eickmeier, S., and Prieto, E. (2010) *Macroeconomic Factors and Micro-level Bank Risk* (Discussion Paper No 20/2010). Deutsche Bundesbank, Frankfurt, Germany.

Campbell, A. (1997) Stakeholders, the case in favour. *Long Range Planning*, **30**, 446–9.

Cao, L. (2007) Efficiency evaluation of China's commercial banks based on super-efficiency model. Paper presented at *Sixth Wuhan International Conference on E-business, 26–27 May 2007, Wuhan, China*.

Caprio Jr, G., and Levine, R. (2002) Corporate governance of banks: concepts and international observations. Paper presented at *Global Corporate Governance Forum Research Network Meeting*.

Carbo-Valverde, S., Humphrey, D., Mandos, J., and Molyneux, P. (2009) Cross-country comparisons of competition and pricing power in European Banking. *Journal of International Money and Finance*, **28**, 115–34.

Carletti, E. (2005) *Competition and Regulation in Banking*. Center for Financial Studies, Frankfurt, Germany.

Casu, B., and Girardone, C. (2009) Competition issues in European banking. *Journal of Financial Regulation and Compliance*, **17**, 119–33.

Casu, B., and Molyneux, P. (2003) A comparative study of efficiency in European banking. *Applied Economics*, **35**, 1865–76.

Caves, D.W., Christensen, L.R., and Diewert, W.E. (1982) The economic theory of index numbers and the measurement of input, output and productivity. *Econometrica*, **50**, 1393–414.

CBRC (2011) *Annual Report*. China Banking Regulatory Commission, Beijing.

CC (1992) *Report of the Cadbury Committee on the Financial Aspects of Corporate Governance*. Gee Publishing, London.

Chaganti, R.S., Mahajan, V., and Sharma, S. (1985) Corporate board size, composition and corporate failure in retail industry. *Journal of Management Studies*, **22**, 400–17.

Chan, Y.S., Greenbaum, S., and Thakor, A. (1986) Information reusability, competition and bank asset quality. *Journal of Banking and Finance*, **10**, 243–53.

Charnes, A., Cooper, W.W., and Rhodes, E. (1978) Measuring the efficiency of decision making units. *European Journal of Operational Research*, **2**(6), 429–44.

Charnes, A., Cooper, W.W., Lewin, A.Y., and Seiford, L.M. (1995) *Data Envelopment Analysis: Theory, Methodology and Applications*. Kluwer, Boston, MA.

Chen, X., Skully, B., and Brown, K. (2005) Banking efficiency in China: application of DEA to pre- and post-deregulation eras: 1993–2000. *China Economic Review*, **16**, 229–45.

Claessens, S., and Laeven, L. (2004) What drives bank competition? Some international evidence. *Journal of Money, Credit and Banking*, **36**, 563–84.

Clark, J.M. (1916) The changing basis of economic responsibility. *Journal of Political Economy*, **24**(3), 209–29.

Clarkson, M.B.E. (1994) *A Risk Based Model of Stakeholder Theory*. Center for Corporate Social Performance and Ethics, University of Toronto, Canada.

Clarkson, M.B.E. (1995) A stakeholder framework for analyzing and evaluating corporate social performance. *Academy of Management Review*, **20**(1), 92–117.

Coccorese, P. (2004) Banking competition and macroeconomic conditions: a disaggregate analysis. *International Journal of Financial Markets, Institutions and Money*, **14**, 203–19.

Coelli, T. (1996) *A Guide to DEAP Version 2.1: A Data Envelopment Analysis (Computer) Program* (CEPA Working Paper No. 1996/08). Center for European Policy Analysis, Washington, DC.

Coelli, T., Prasada Rao, D.S., and Battese, G.E. (1998) *An Introduction to Efficiency and Productivity Analysis*. Kluwer Academic Publishers, Norwell, MA.

Davis, J.H., Schoorman, F.D., and Donaldson, L. (1997) Toward a stewardship theory of management. *Academy of Management Review*, **22**(1), 20–47.

De Bandt, O., and Davis, E.P. (2000) Competition, contestability and market structure in European banking sectors on the eve of EMU. *Journal of Banking and Finance*, **24**, 1045–1066.

Debreu, G. (1951) The coefficient of resource utilization. *Econometrica*, **19**, 273–92.

Degryse, H., Kim, M., and Ongena, S. (2009) *Microeconometrics of Banking*. Oxford University Press, Oxford, UK.

Delis, M., Molyneux, P., and Pasiouras, F. (2011) Regulations and productivity growth in banking: evidence from transition economies. *Journal of Money, Credit and Banking*, **43**, 735–64.

Dell'Ariccia, G., and Marquez, R. (2006) Lending booms and lending standards. *Journal of Finance*, **61**(5), 2511–46.

Demirguc-Kunt, A., and Huizinga, H. (1999a) *Market Discipline and Financial Safety Net Design* (Policy Research Paper No. 2183). World Bank, Washington, D.C.

Demirguc-Kunt, A., and Huizinga, H. (1999b) Determinants of commercial bank interest margins and profitability: some international evidence. *World Bank Economic Review*, **13**(2), 379–408.

Demirguc-Kunt, A., and Huizinga, H. (2010) Bank activity and funding strategies: the impact on risk and return. *Journal of Financial Economics*, **98**(3), 626–50.

Demirguc-Kunt, A., and Peria, M.S.M. (2010) *A Framework for Analyzing Competition in the Banking Sector: An Application to the Case of Jordan* (Policy Research Working Paper No. 5499). World Bank, Washington, DC, pp. 1–24.

Diamond, D.W., and Dybvig, P. (1983) Bank runs, deposit insurance, and liquidity. *Journal of Political Economy*, **91**(3), 401–19.

Dietrich, A., and Wanzenried, G. (2011) Determinants of bank profitability before and during the crisis: evidence from Switzerland. *Journal of International Financial Markets, Institutions and Money*, **21**(3), 307–27.

Dodd, E.M. (1932) For whom are corporate managers trustees? *Harvard Law Review*, **45**, 1145–63.

Donaldson, L. (1990) The ethereal hand, organisational economies and management theory. *Academy of Management Review*, **15**(3), 369–81.

Donaldson, T., and Davis, J.H. (1991) Agency theory and stewardship theory: CEO governance and shareholder returns. *Australian Journal of Management*, **16**, 49–64.

Donaldson, T., and Preston, L. (1995) The stakeholder theory of the corporation: concepts, evidence, implications. *Academy of Management Review*, **20**, 69–91.

Doucouliagos, C. (1994) A note on the evolution of *Homo economicus*. *Journal of Economics Issues*, **3**, 877–83.

EBF (2012) *EU Banking Sector Facts and Figures*. European Banking Federation, Brussels, Belgium.

Eichengreen, B., and Gibson, H.D (2001) *Greek Banking at the Dawn of the New Millennium* (CEPR Discussion Paper No. 2791). Centre for Economic Policy Research, London.

Eisenhardt, K.M. (1989) Agency theory: an assessment and review. *Academy of Management Review*, **14**(1), 57–74.

Fama, E., and Jensen, M. (1983a) Separation of ownership and control. *Journal of Law and Economics*, **26**(2), 301–25.

Fama, E., and Jensen, M. (1983b) Agency problems and residual claims. *Journal of Law and Economics*, **26**(2), 327–49.

Fang, Y., Hasan, I., and Marton, K. (2011) *Market Reforms, Legal Changes and Bank Risk-taking: Evidence from Transition Economies* (Bank of Finland Discussion Paper No. 7). Bank of Finland, Helsinki.

Fare, R., Grosskopf, S., and Weber, W.L. (2004) The effect of risk-based capital requirements on profits efficiency in banking. *Applied Economics*, **36**, 1731–43.

Farrell, M.J. (1957) The measurement of productive efficiency. *Journal of the Royal Statistical Society*, **120**(3), 253–90.

Fernandez de Guevara, J., Mandos, J., and Perez, F. (2005) Market power in European banking. *Journal of Financial Services Research*, **27**, 109–37.

Ferrier, G., and Lovell, C.A.K. (1990) Measuring cost efficiency in banking: econometric and linear programming evidence. *Journal of Econometrics*, **46**, 229–45.

Finkelstein, S., and D'Aveni, R.A. (1994) CEO duality as a double-edged sword: how boards of directors balance entrenchment avoidance and unity of command. *Academy of Management Journal*, **37**, 1079–1108.

Fleischer, A., Hazard, G.C.,and Klipper, M.Z. (1988) *Board Games: The Changing Shape of Corporate Power*. Little, Brown & Co., Boston, MA.

Fligstein, N., and Freeland, R. (1995) Theoretical and comparative perspectives on corporate organization. *Annual Review of Sociology*, **21**, 21–43.

Freeman, R.E. (1984) *Strategic Management: A Stakeholder Approach*. Pitman, Boston, MA.

Friedman, A., and Miles, S. (2002) Developing stakeholder theory. *Journal of Management Studies*, **39**, 1–21.

Fries, S., and Taci, A. (2005) Cost efficiency of banks in transition: evidence from 289 banks in 15 post-communist countries. *Journal of Banking and Finance*, **29**(1), 55–81.

Fu, M. (2009) Competition in Chinese commercial banking. *Banking and Finance Review*, **1**, 1–16.

Fu, X., and Heffernan, S. (2007) Cost X-efficiency in China's banking sector. *China Economic Review*, **18**, 35–53.

Garcia-Herrero, A., Gavila, S., and Santabarbara, D. (2009) What explains the low profitability of Chinese banks? *Journal of Banking and Finance*, **33**, 2080–92.

Garcia-Marco, T., and Robles-Fernandez, M.D. (2008) Risk-taking behaviour and ownership in the banking industry: the Spanish evidence. *Journal of Economics and Business*, **60**, 332–54.

Garten, H.A. (1986) Banking on the market: relying on depositors to control bank risk. *Yale Journal on Regulation*, **4**, 129–34.

Garza-Garcia, J.G. (2012) Determinants of bank efficiency in Mexico: a two-stage analysis. *Applied Economics Letters*, **19**, 1679–82.

Gerschenkron, A. (1962) *Economic Backwardness in Historical Perspective*. Belknap Press, Cambridge, MA.

Girardone, C., Molyneux, P., and Gardener, E.P.M. (2004) Analysing the determinants of bank efficiency: the case of Italian banks. *Applied Economics*, **36**, 215–27.

Goddard, J., Molyneux, P., and Wilson, J (2004) Dynamic of growth and profitability in banking. *Journal of Money, Credit and Banking*, **36**(6), 1069–90.

Goddard, J., Molyneux, P., Liu, H., and Wilson, J. (2011) The persistence of bank profit. *Journal of Banking and Finance*, **35**, 2881–90.

Graham, C., and Bordelean, E (2010) *The Impact of Liquidity on Bank Profitability* (Working Paper No. 2010-38). Bank of Canada, Ottawa.

Greenwald, B., and Stiglitz, J.E. (1986) Externlities in economies with imperfect information and incomplete markets. *Quarterly Journal of Economics*, **101**, 229–64.

Griliches, Z. (1987) Productivity: measurement problems. In: J. Eatwell, M. Milgate, and P. Newman (Eds), *The New Palgrave Dictionary of Economics*. Palgrave Macmillan, Basingstoke, UK.

Guru, B., Staunton, J., and Balashanmugam, B (2002) Determinants of commercial bank profitability in Malaysia. Paper presented at *12th Annual Australian Finance and Banking Conference, 16–17 December 2002, Sydney, Australia.*

Hanna, T., and Hanweck, G.A. (1988) Bank insolvency risk and the market for large certificates of deposits. *Journal of Money, Credit and Banking*, **20**(2), 203–11.

Hart, O., Shleifer, A., and Vishny, R. (1997) The proper scope of government: theory and an application to prisons. *Quarterly Journal of Economics*, **112**, 1127–62.

Hasan, I., and Xie, R. (2012) *A Note on Foreign Bank Entry and Bank Corporate Governance in China* (BOFIT Discussion Paper No. 8/2012). Bank of Finland, Helsinki.

Hassan, M.K., and Bashir, A.H.M. (2003) Determinants of islamic banking profitability. Paper presented at *Tenth ERF Annual Conference, Morocco.*

Heffernan, S.A. (1996) *Modern Banking in Theory and Practice*. John Wiley & Sons, Chichester, UK.

Heffernan, S., and Fu, M. (2010) Determinants of financial performance in Chinese banking. *Applied Financial Economics*, **20**(20), 1585–1600.

Herring, R.J., and Carmassi, J. (2010) The corporate structure of international financial conglomerates: complexity and its implications for safety and soundness. In: A.N. Berger, P. Molyneux, and J.O.S. Wilson (Eds), *Oxford Handbook of Banking*. Oxford University Press, Oxford, UK.

Hesse, H., and Cihak, M. (2007) *Competitive Banks and Financial Stability* (Working Paper No. 07/02). International Monetary Fund, Washington, DC.

Hill, C.W., and Jones, T.M. (1992) Stakeholder–agency theory. *Journal of Management Studies*, **29**, 131–54.

Houston, J., and James, C. (1995) CEO compensation and bank risk: Is compensation in banking structured to promote risk taking? *Journal of Monetary Economics*, **36**, 405–31.

Hu, J.L., Chu, W.K., Hu, X.L., and Lee, C.Y. (2009) Operational environment-adjusted nationwide bank efficiency in China. *Journal of Management Research*, **9**, 142–58.

Iannotta, G., Nocera, G., and Sirono, A. (2007) Ownership structure, risk and performance in the European banking industry. *Journal of Banking and Finance*, **31**, 2127–49.

Jeitschko, T.D., and Jeung, S.D. (2005) Incentives for risk-taking in banking: a unified approach. *Journal of Banking and Finance*, **29**, 759–77.

Jensen, M.C., and Meckling, W.H. (1976) Theory of firms: managerial behaviour, agency cost and ownership. *Journal of Financial Economics*, **3**, 305–60.

Jensen, M.C., and Murphy, K. (1990) Performance pay and top-management incentives. *Journal of Political Economy*, **98**, 225–64.

Jiang, C.X., Yao, S.J., and Zhang, Z.Y. (2009) The effects of governance changes on bank efficiency in China: a stochastic distance function approach. *China Economic Review*, **20**, 717–31.

Jiang, G., Tang, N., Law, E., and Sze, A (2003) *Determinants of Bank Profitability in Hong Kong* (Research Memorandum, September). Hong Kong Monetary Authority, Hong Kong, China.

Jones, T.M. (1995) Instrumental stakeholder theory: a synthesis of ethics and economics. *Academy of Management Review*, **20**, 404–37.

Jorgenson, D., and Griliches, Z. (1967) The explanation of productivity change. *Review of Economic Studies*, **89**, 109–15.

Judson, R.A., and Owen, A.L. (1999) Estimating dynamic panel data models: a guide for macroeconomics. *Economics Letters*, **65**, 9–15.

Keasey, K., and Wright, M. (1993) Issues in corporate accountability and governance. *Accounting and Business Research*, **91a**, 291–303.

Keeley, M.C. (1990) Deposit insurance, risk and market power in banking. *American Economic Review*, **80**, 1183–1200.

Koopmans, T.C. (1951) An analysis of production as an efficient combination of activities. In: T.C. Koopmans (Ed.), *Activity Analysis of Production and Allocation*. John Wiley & Sons, New York.

Kosmidou, K., Pasiouras, F., Doumpos, M., and Zopounidis, C. (2006) Assessing performance factors in the UK banking sector: a multicriteria methodology. *Central European Journal of Operations Research*, **1**, 25–44.

Kumbhakar, S.C., and Wang D. (2007) Economic reforms, efficiency and productivity in Chinese banking. *Journal of Regulatory Economics*, **32**, 105–29.

Laffont, J.J., and Tirole, J. (1993) *A Theory of Incentives in Regulation and Procurement*. MIT Press, Cambridge, MA.

Laurenceson, J., and Zhao, Y. (2008) Efficiency amongst China's banks: a DEA analysis five years after WTO entry. *China Economic Journal*, **1**, 275–85.

Learmount, S. (2004) *Corporate Governance: What Can Be Learned from Japan?* Oxford University Press, Oxford, UK.

Lerner, A.P. (1934) The concept of monopoly and the measurement of monopoly power. *Review of Economic Studies*, **1**, 157–75.

Levine, R. (2003) *The Corporate Governance of Banks: A Concise Discussion of Concepts and Evidence* (Policy Research Working Paper No. 3404). World Bank, Washington, D.C.

Lin, X.X., and Zhang, Y. (2009) Bank ownership reform and bank performance in China. *Journal of Banking and Finance*, **33**(1), 20–9.

Liu, H., and Wilson, J.O.S. (2013) Competition and risk in Japanese banking. *European Journal of Finance*, **19**(1), 1–18.

Liu, H., Molyneux, P., and Wilson, J.O.S. (2013) Competition and stability in European banking: a regional analysis. *The Manchester School*, **81**(2), 176–201.

Lovell, C.A.K., Wallers, L.C., and Wood, L.L. (1995) Stratified models of education production using modified DEA and regression analysis. In: A. Charnes, W.W. Cooper, A.Y. Lewin, and L.M. Seiford (Eds), *Data Envelopment Analysis: Theory, Methodology and Application*. Kluwer Academic Publishers, Norwell, MA, pp. 329–52.

Lown, C., and Morgan, D.P. (2006) The credit cycle and the business cycle: new findings using the loan officer opinion survey. *Journal of Money, Credit and Banking*, **38**(6), 1575–97.

Macey, J.R., and O'Hara, M. (2003) The corporate governance of banks. *Economic Policy Review*, April, 91–107.

Marcus, A.J. (1984) Deregulation and bank financial policy. *Journal of Banking and Finance*, **8**, 557–65.

Martinez-Miera, D., and Repullo, R. (2010) Does competition reduce the risk of bank failure? *Review of Financial Studies*, **23**, 3638–64.

Masood, O., and Sergi, B.S. (2011) China's banking system, market structure and competitive conditions. *Frontier of Economics in China*, **6**(1), 22–35.

Matthews, K., Murinde, V., and Zhao, T. (2007) Competitive conditions among the major British banks. *Journal of Banking and Finance*, **31**, 2025–42.

Maudos, J., and Fernandez de Guevara, J. (2004) Factors explaining the evolution of the interest margin in the banking sectors of the European Union. *Journal of Banking and Finance*, **28**(9), 2259–81.

Maudos, J., Pastor, J.M., Perez, F., and Quesada, J. (2002) Cost and profit efficiency in European banks. *Journal of International Financial Markets, Institutions and Money*, **12**, 33–58.

McConnell, J.J., and Servaes, H. (1990) Additional evidence on equity ownership and corporate value. *Journal of Financial Economics*, **27**, 595–612.

Meeusen, W., and Van den Broeck, J. (1977) Efficiency estimation from Cobb–Douglas production functions with composed error. *International Economic Review*, **18**, 435–44.

Mensi, S (2010) Measurement of competitiveness degree in Tunisian deposit banks: an application of the Panzar and Rosse model. *Panoeconomicus*, **2**, 189–207.

Mishkin, F.S. (1999) Financial consolidation: dangers and opportunities. *Journal of Banking and Finance*, **23**, 675–91.

Molyneux, P. (1993) Structure and performance in European banking. Doctoral dissertation, University of Wales, Bangor, UK.

Molyneux, P., and Thornton, J (1992) Determinants of European bank profitability: a note. *Journal of Banking and Finance*, **16**, 1173–8.

Molyneux, P., Lloyd-Williams, D.M., and Thornton, J. (1994) Competitive conditions in European banking. *Journal of Banking and Finance*, **18**, 445–59.

Molz, R. (1988) Managerial domination of boards of directors and financial performance. *Journal of Business Research*, **16**, 235–49.

Monks, R.A.G., and Minow, N. (1995) *Corporate Governance*. Blackwell, Malden, MA.

Moran, P., and Ghoshal, S. (1996) Theories of economic organisation: the case for realism and balance. *American Economic Review*, **21**(1), 58–72.

Morck, R., Shleifer, A., and Vishny, R.W. (1988) Management ownership and market valuation: an empirical analysis. *Journal of Financial Economics*, **20**, 293–315.

Negrin, J.L., Enrique, B., Diadelfa, O., and Pedro, S. (2006) Competition in the Mexican banking system 2000–2005: a disaggregated analysis. Paper presented at *Meeting of Latin American and Caribbean Economic Association (LACEA) and Latin American Meeting of the Econometric Society (LAMES), 2–4 November 2006.*

OECD (1999) *Principles of Corporate Governance*. Organisation for Economic Co-operation and Development, Paris.

Park, K.H. (2013) Testing for competition in the South Korean and Chinese commercial banking markets. *Asia-Pacific Journal of Financial Studies*, **42**, 56–75.

Park, Y.C. (1991) Financial repression and liberalization. In: L.B. Krause and K. Kihwan (Eds), *Liberalization in the Process of Economic Development*. University of California Press, Oxford, UK.

Pasiouras, F., and Kosmidou, K. (2007) Factors influencing the profitability of domestic and foreign commercial banks in the European Union. *Research in International Business and Finance*, **21**(2), 222–37.

Perrow, C. (1986) *Complex Organization*. Random House, New York.

Perry, P. (1992) Do banks gain or lose from inflation? *Journal of Retail Banking*, **14**(2), 25–30.

Prowse, S. (1997) The corporate governance system in banking: What do we know? *Banca Nazionale del Lavoro Quarterly Review*, March, 11–40.

Rochet, J.C. (1992) Capital requirements and the behaviour of commercial banks. *European Economic Review*, **36**, 1137–78.

Rojas, C. (2011) Market power and the Lerner index: a classroom experiment. *Journal of Industrial Organization Education*, **5**, 1–19.

Roodman, D. (2006) *How to Do xtabond2: An Introduction to Difference and System GMM in Stata* (Working Paper No. 103). Centre for Global Development, Washington, DC.

Ross, S. (1973) The economic theory of agency: the principal's problem. *American Economic Review*, **63**, 134–9.

Saez, L., and Shi, L. (2004) Liquidity pools, risk sharing and financial contagion. *Journal of Financial Services Research*, **25**, 5–23.

Shaffer, S. (1982) Non-structural test for competition in financial markets. Paper presented at *Conference on Bank Structure and Competition, Chicago, 1982*. Federal Reserve Bank of Chicago, Chicago, IL, pp. 225–33.

Shleifer, A., and Vishny, R.W. (1997) A survey of corporate governance. *Journal of Finance*, **52**, 737–83.

Short, H., and Keasey, K. (1999) Managerial ownership and the performance of firms: evidence from the UK. *Journal of Corporate Finance*, **5**, 79–101.

Smirlock, M (1985) Evidence on the (non) relationship between concentration and profitability in banking. *Journal of Money, Credit, and Banking*, **17**, 69–83.

Smith, A. (1976) *An Inquiry into the Nature and Causes of the Wealth of Nations*. University of Chicago Press, Chicago, IL.

Solow, R.M. (1957) Technical change and the aggregate production function. *Review of Economics and Statistics*, **39**, 312–20.

Staikouras, C., and Wood, G. (2003) The determinants of bank profitability in Europe. Paper presented at *European Applied Business Research Conference, 9–13 June 2003, Venice, Italy.*

Stern, G.H., and Feldman, R.J. (2004) *Too Big to Fail: The Hazards of Bank Bailouts*. Brooking Institution Press, Washington, DC.

Stigler, G.J. (1947) *Trends in Output and Eemployment*. National Bureau of Economic Research, New York.

Stiglitz, J.E. (1993) The role of the state in financial markets. *Proceedings of the World Bank Annual Conference on Economic Development*, pp. 19–56.

Stiglitz, J.E., and Weiss, A. (1981) Credit rationing in markets with imperfect information. *American Economic Review*, **71**, 393–410.

Stiroh, K.J. (2010) Diversification in banking. In: A. Berger, P. Molyneux, and J.O.S. Wilson (Ed.), *Oxford Handbook of Banking*. Oxford University Press, Oxford, UK.

Sufian, F. (2009a) Determinants of bank profitability in a developing economy: empirical evidence from the China banking sector. *Journal of Asia-Pacific Business*, **10**(4), 201–307.

Sufian, F. (2009b) Analysis of the relevance of non-traditional activities items upon the efficiency of Chinese banks: a non-stochastic frontier DEA approach. *Review of Economic and Business Studies*, **4**, 83–102.

Sufian, F., and Habibullah, M.S. (2009) Bank specific and macroeconomic determinants of bank profitability: empirical evidence from the China banking sector. *Frontiers of Economics in China*, **4**(2), 274–91.

Sufian, F., and Habibullah, M.S. (2010) Bank-specific, industry-specific and macroeconomic determinants of bank efficiency: empirical evidence from the Thai banking sector. *Journal of Applied Economic Research*, **4**, 427–61.

Sufian, F., and Majid, M.A.Z. (2009) Bank efficiency and share prices in China: empirical evidence from a three-stage model. *International Journal of Computational Economics and Econometrics*, **1**, 23–45.

Tan, Y., and Floros, C. (2012a) Bank profitability and inflation: the case of China. *Journal of Economic Studies*, **39**(6), 675–96.

Tan, Y., and Floros, C. (2012b) Bank profitability and GDP growth in China: a note. *Journal of Chinese Economics and Business Studies*, **10**(3), 267–73.

Tan, Y., and Floros, C. (2014) Risk, profitability and competition: evidence from the Chinese banking industry. *Journal of Developing Areas*, **48**, 303–19.

Tinbergen, J. (1942) On the theory of trend movements. In: L.H. Klaasen, L.M. Joyck, and H.J. Witteveen (Eds.), *Jan Tinbergen, Selected Papers*. North-Holland, Amsterdam, pp. 182–221.

Tirole, J. (1994) The internal organization of governments. *Oxford Economic Papers*, **46**, 1–29.

Tricker, R.I. (1994) *International Corporate Governance*. Simon & Schuster, Singapore.

Triole, J. (1987) *The Theory of Industrial Organization*. MIT Press, Cambridge, MA.

Vesala, J. (1995) *Testing for Competition in Banking: Behavioral Evidence from Finland* (Bank of Finland Study No. E1). Bank of Finland, Helsinki.

Waldo, C.N. (1985) *Boards of Directors: Their Changing Roles, Structure and Information Needs*. Quorum Books, Westport, CT.

WB (1999) Corporate governance: framework for implementation. Available from: *http://www.worldbank.org/* [World Bank].

Weill, L. (2003) Banking efficiency in transition economies: the role of foreign ownership. *Economics of Transition*, **11**, 569–92.

Xu, B., Rixtel, A.N., and Leuvensteijn, M.V. (2013) *Measuring Bank Competition in China: A Comparison of New versus Conventional Approaches Applied to Loan Markets* (BIS Working Paper No. 422). Bank for International Settlements, Basel, Switzerland.

Yao, S., Jiang, C., Feng, G., and Willenbockel, D. (2007) On the efficiency of Chinese banks and WTO challenges. *Applied Economics*, **39**, 629–43.

Yermack, D. (1995) Do corporations award CEO stock options effectively? *Journal of Financial Economics*, **39**, 237–69.

Yuan, Y. (2006) The state of competition of Chinese banking industry. *Journal of Asian Economics*, **17**, 519–34.

Index

Page numbers in *italics* refer to figures and those in **bold** refer to tables.

FSC
www.fsc.org
MIX
Papier | Fördert gute Waldnutzung
FSC® C083411

Kolibri 360 GmbH
Ferdinand-Jühlke-Straße 7
99095 Erfurt, Deutschland
produktsicherheit@kolibri360.de